The Ultimate Bible Trivia Book for Teens

600 Fun-Filled Questions to Test Your Knowledge, Challenge Friends, and Grow Your Faith

Welcome Aboard, Check Out This Limited-Time Free Bonus!

Ahoy, reader! Welcome to the Ahoy Publications family, and thanks for snagging a copy of this book! Since you've chosen to join us on this journey, we'd like to offer you something special.

Check out the link below for a FREE e-book filled with delightful facts about American History.

But that's not all - you'll also have access to our exclusive email list with even more free e-books and insider knowledge. Well, what are ye waiting for? Click the link below to join and set sail toward exciting adventures in American History.

Access your bonus here
https://ahoypublications.com/
Or, Scan the QR code!

Table of Contents

Section 1: Genesis - Revelation

Part 1: The Beginning: Way Back When It All Started

Genesis talks about creation, the first people on Earth, and how the stage was set for a Biblical journey. Let's jump right into how it all began.

Multiple Choice Missions:

1. According to the first book of the Bible, what was the first thing God created?

    a) The sun, moon, and stars

    b) Land

    c) Light

    d) Plants and trees

2. What was the name of the special garden where God placed Adam and Eve?

    a) Zion

    b) Eden

    c) Canaan

    d) Galilee

3. There was one tree that God told Adam and Eve not to eat from. Which one was it?

    a) The Tree of Life

    b) The Tree of the Knowledge of Good and Evil

    c) The Tree of Healing

    d) The Tree of Wisdom

4. Who was it that convinced Eve to go against God's command?

    a) An angel

    b) A lion

    c) The serpent

    d) A bird

5. What was the very first thing Adam and Eve realized about themselves right after they ate the forbidden fruit?

    a) They instantly received divine wisdom.

    b) Their eyes were opened, and they realized they were naked.

    c) They could now understand and speak every animal's language.

    d) They were made immune to aging and death.

True or False:

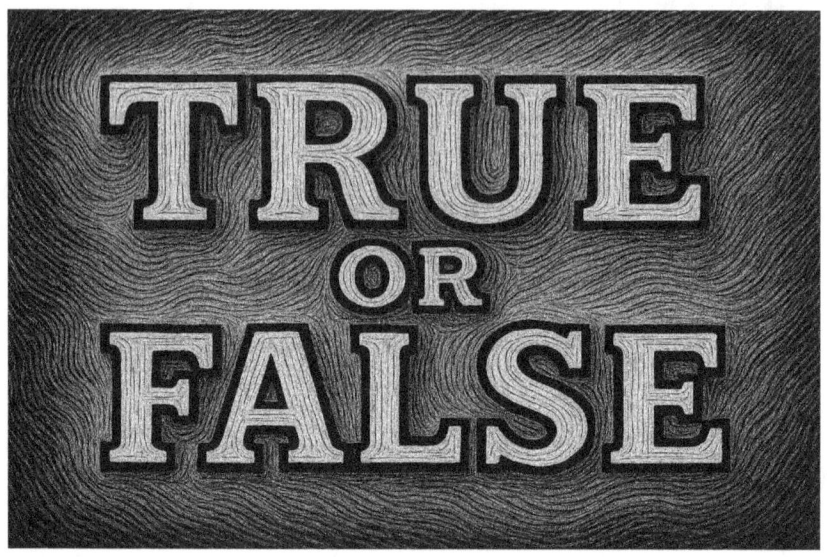

6. True or False: Cain was the older brother of Abel.

7. True or False: Abel offered vegetables as a gift to God.

8. True or False: God was happy with the gift that Cain brought.

9. True or False: Cain killed his brother Abel because he was jealous and angry.

10. True or False: After killing Abel, Cain was not punished by God.

Fill in the Blank:

11. The Bible says that God created humans in His own _____.

12. After creating everything, God rested on the _____ day.

13. The serpent told the first woman that if she ate the fruit, she would become like _____.

14. To guard the way to the Tree of Life after they were sent out of the garden, God placed _____ at the east of Eden.

15. As a punishment for what he did to his brother, Cain was made to be a restless _____ on the earth.

Who Said That?

16. "Am I my brother's keeper?" Who said this?

    a) The first man

    b) The first woman

    c) Cain

    d) Abel

17. "Let there be light." Who said these powerful words?

    a) The first man

    b) God

    c) The Serpent

    d) An angel

Bible Book Breakdown:

18. When Adam had lived 130 years, he had a son called _____.

19. After his son was born, Adam lived for f _____ more years and had other sons and daughters.

Answers

Multiple Choice Missions

1. c) Light

2. b) Eden

3. b) The Tree of the Knowledge of Good and Evil

4. c) A serpent

5.b) Their eyes were opened, and they realized they were naked.

True or False:

6. True

7. False

8. False

9. True

10. False

Fill in the Blank

11. Image

12. Seventh

13. God

14. Cherubim

15. Wanderer

Who Said That?

16. c) Cain

17. b) God

Bible Book Breakdown:

18. Seth

19. 800

Part 2: Noah's Epic Voyage & The Tower That Tried Too Hard!

After the Garden of Eden, several noteworthy events followed, such as a massive flood and a tower with a plan so ambitious it is still known today. Ready to see what you know about Noah's epic boat trip and the Tower of Babel?

Multiple Choice Missions:

1. In Genesis, we see that the world had become pretty messed up, but there was one guy God saw who was living right. Who was he?

    a) Cain's great-great-great-grandson

    b) Methuselah

    c) Noah

    d) Abraham

2. What kind of boat did God tell Noah to build?

    a) A reed boat for river travel

    b) A sturdy merchant ship for trading

    c) A massive wooden ark to preserve life (Noah, his family and the animals on board)

3. How did God get all the animals onto the ark?

    a) Noah had to go out and round them all up.

    b) They showed up on their own in pairs.

    c) The animals were led to the ark by God.

    d) Only certain types of animals were allowed.

4. After the flood, what sign did God give Noah to promise that He'd never flood the whole Earth again?

    a) A dove holding a leaf

    b) A loud voice from the sky

    c) A rainbow

    d) A set of stone tablets

5. What big project did people start after the flood, thinking they could build something that reached heaven?

    a) Building a giant staircase

    b) Stacking large rock piles

    c) A super tall tower

True or False:

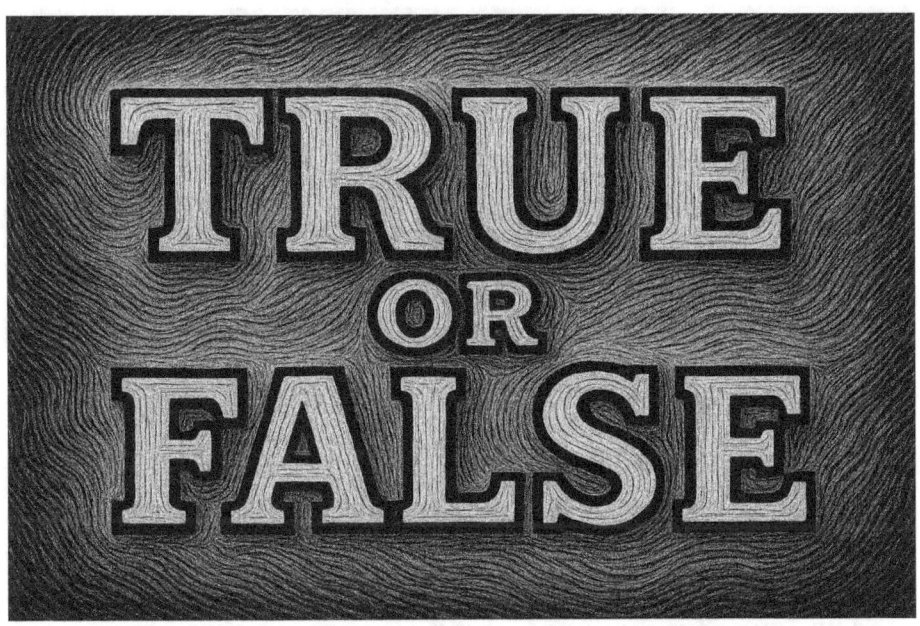

6. True or False: Noah only brought his immediate family onto the ark, together with the animals that were brought inside.

7. True or False: The ark was bigger than any ship we have today.

8. True or False: God was impressed with how united and determined people were to build the Tower of Babel.

9. True or False: The Bible says that because of the Tower of Babel, God made people speak different languages.

10. True or False: The Tower of Babel was finished and reached all the way to Heaven.

Fill in the Blank:

11. God told Noah to build the ark out of _____ wood.

12. Noah sent out _____ to see if the water had gone down.

13. The names of Noah's sons were _____.

14. Before God intervened, everyone building the Tower of Babel spoke the same _____.

15. Because of the tower, God scattered people all over the face of the _____.

Who Said That?

16. "I will never again destroy all living creatures by floodwaters, and never again will there be a flood to destroy the earth." Who made this promise?

    a) Noah

    b) One of Noah's sons

    c) God

    d) Noah's wife

17. "Come, let us build ourselves a city and a tower with its top in the heavens, and let us make a name for ourselves..." What was the main reason behind the Tower of Babel?

    a) To worship God better

    b) To protect themselves from future floods

    c) To glorify themselves and reach Heaven

    d) To see the stars

Bible Book Breakdown:

18. Noah was _____ years old when the floodwater came.

19. According to the Bible, the ark came to rest on the mountains of_____ on the seventeenth day of the seventh month.

Answers:

Multiple Choice Missions

1. c) Noah

2. c) A massive wooden ark to preserve life

3. c) The animals were led to the ark by God.

4. c) A rainbow

5. c) A super tall tower

True or False

6. True

7. False

8. False

9. True

10. False

Fill in the Blank

11. Gopher

12. Dove

13. Shem, Ham, and Japheth

14. Language

15. Earth

Who Said That?

16. c) God

17. c) To make a name for themselves and reach Heaven

Bible Book Breakdown

18. 600

19. Genesis

Part 3: From One Family to a Nation

We're still in Genesis, but the story is now focusing on one family that God chose to do some seriously big things through. Get ready to meet Abraham (originally Abram), his wife Sarah (originally Sarai), their son Isaac, Isaac's son Jacob and Jacob's favorite son, Joseph.

Multiple Choice Missions:

1. God made an incredible promise to Abraham (original name Abram), saying his family would grow to be as many as what?

    a) The number of trees in the forest

    b) The grains of sand on a beach

    c) The stars in the sky

2. What was the seemingly impossible thing that God promised Abraham and Sarah when they were already old?

    a) They would become king and queen.

    b) They would travel to every corner of the world.

    c) They would have a child.

3. What was the name of the son born to Abraham and Sarah in their old age? a) Ishmael

    b) Isaac

    c) Jacob

    d) Joseph

4. God tested Abraham's faith with a really tough request. What was he asked to do with Isaac?

    a) Send him away.

    b) Offer him as a sacrifice.

    c) Make him work on the family farm.

5. Jacob had a famous dream about a stairway (or ladder) reaching up to heaven. What was happening on it?

    a) Angels were sliding down it.

    b) People were climbing up.

    c) Angels were going up and down it.

True or False:

6. True or False: Abraham (Abram) obeyed when God asked him to leave his home.

7. True or False: Sarah (Sarai) always believed God's promise that she would have a child.

8. True or False: Isaac was Abraham's only son.

9. True or False: Jacob tricked his brother Esau out of some important family rights and a blessing.

10. True or False: Joseph's brothers sold him into slavery because they thought his dreams were cool.

Fill in the Blank:

11. God made a special agreement with Abraham, and it was marked by an act of _____.

12. Abraham's original home was in the land of _____.

13. Jacob wrestled with _____ and his name was changed to Israel.

14. God allowed Joseph to interpret_____.

15. In the end, Joseph became a powerful leader in the nation of _____.

Who Said That?

16. "Here I am," Abraham replied. Who was he talking to?

   a) Isaac

   b) Sarah

   c) God

17. "Look, it's still broad daylight; it's not time for the animals to be gathered. Water the sheep and take them back to pasture." Who said this?

   a) Jacob

   b) Leah

   c) Laban

   d) Isaac

Bible Book Breakdown:

18. The Medianites sold Joseph to _____ in Egypt.

19. Joseph told the chief cupbearer his dream of the vine with the three branches meant _____.

Answers

Multiple Choice Missions

1. c) The stars in the sky

2. c) They would have a child.

3. b) Isaac

4. b) Offer him as a sacrifice.

5. c) Angels were going up and down it.

True or False

6. True

7. False

8. False

9. True

10. False

Fill in the Blank

11. Circumcision

12. Ur

13. God

14. Dreams

15. Egypt

Who Said That?

16. c) God

17. a) Jacob

Bible Book Breakdown

18. Potiphar

19. He would be reinstated in his position in three days.

Part 4: From Slavery to Exodus - Let My People Go!

From here, the story gets really serious. The family of Abraham, Isaac, and Jacob has grown into a huge group of people in Egypt, but they were now slaves. Although things looked pretty bad, God had a plan, involving a man named Moses. Get ready for burning bushes, plagues, and an escape that changed everything.

Multiple Choice Missions:

1. Why did the Pharaoh of Egypt make the Israelites slaves?

    a) They weren't following his rules.

    b) He was worried they'd grow too numerous and powerful.

    c) He wanted all their belongings.

2. How did God first get Moses' attention?

    a) Through a whisper in the wind.

    b) In a dream.

    c) Through a burning bush that wasn't burning up.

    d) By sending a messenger.

3. What did God tell Moses to demand from Pharaoh?

    a) Land for his people.

    b) To make his people rich.

    c) That the Israelites be allowed to leave with all their belongings.

4. Which one of these was NOT one of the plagues God sent upon Egypt?

    a) Locusts

    b) Darkness

    c) Massive Floods

    d) Frogs

5. What was the really terrible plague that finally made Pharaoh let the Israelites leave?

    a) Famine.

    b) Death of all the farm animals.

    c) The firstborn son in every Egyptian family died.

True or False:

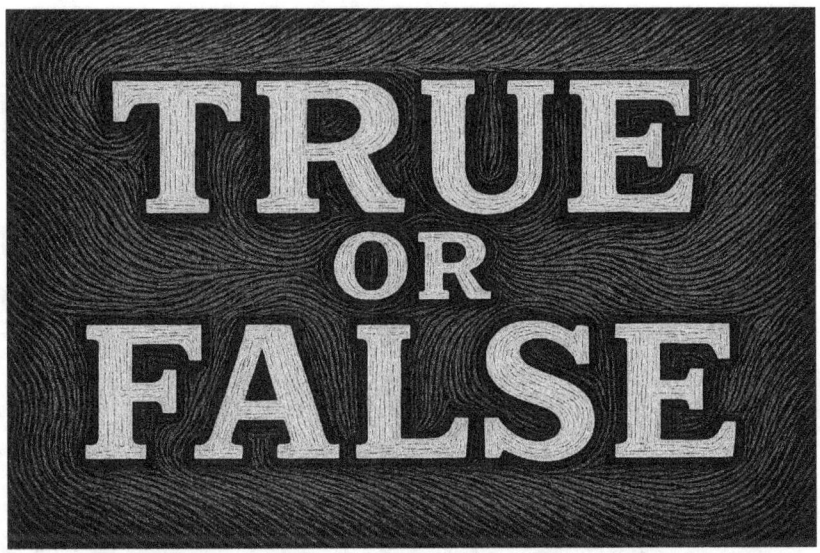

6. True or False: Moses was super excited and felt totally ready to lead the Israelites out of Egypt from the beginning.
7. True or False: Pharaoh let the Israelites go after the very first plague.
8. True or False: The Israelites baked bread without yeast because they had to leave Egypt super fast.
9. True or False: God split apart the water of the Red Sea so the Israelites could walk across on dry land.
10. True or False: Pharaoh himself led his army to chase after the Israelites but decided to turn around before they reached the sea.

Fill in the Blank:

11. Moses' brother, _____, helped him speak to Pharaoh.
12. The festival commemorating when the Israelites left Egypt, after the plague of death on the firstborn, is called _____.
13. God guided the Israelites through the desert with a pillar of _____ during the day and a pillar of _____ at night.
14. The mountain where Moses received the Ten Commandments is called Mount _____.
15. The special tent where the Israelites worshipped God in the desert was called the _____.

Who Said That?

16. "Let my people go, so that they may worship Me in the wilderness." Who was asked to give this message to Pharaoh?

    a) Aaron

    b) Moses

    c) Miriam

Bible Book Breakdown:

17. Moses' wife and the mother of his sons Gershom and Eliezer was called _____.

18. Moses was _____ years old when he died.

Answers

Multiple Choice Missions

1. b) He was worried they'd grow too numerous and powerful.

2. c) Through a burning bush that wasn't burning up.

3. c) That the Israelites be allowed to leave with all their belongings.

4. c) Massive Floods

5. c) The firstborn son in every Egyptian family died.

True or False

6. False

7. False

8. True

9. True

10. False

Fill in the Blank

11. Aaron

12. Passover

13. Cloud, Fire

14. Sinai

15. Tabernacle

Who Said That?

16. b) Moses

Bible Book Breakdown

17. Zipporah

18. 120

Part 5: Wilderness Wanderings & The Promised Land - The Ultimate Road Trip (With Detours!)

After God's powerful deliverance from Egypt, the Israelites faced a challenging journey to the Promised Land. Their wilderness experience was a spiritual proving ground filled with incredible miracles like food sent from heaven, but also marked by significant complaints and disobedience. Here, we'll explore their time learning God's laws, including the Ten Commandments, as they endured their wanderings before finally stepping into the inheritance God had planned for them

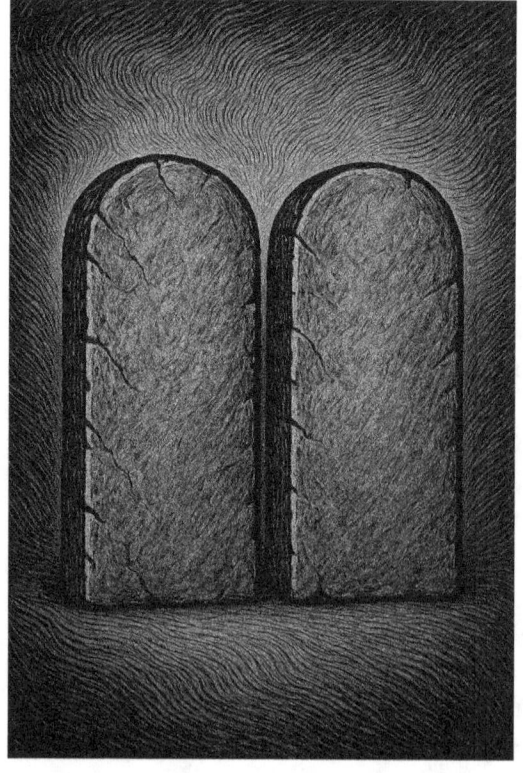

Multiple Choice Missions:

1. What kind of food did God miraculously provide for the Israelites in the desert?

    a) Fruit

    b) Manna

    c) Vegetables

    d) Sunflower seeds

2. According to biblical accounts, what three items were kept inside the Ark of the Covenant?

    a) A golden cup, a scroll of Isaiah, and a bronze serpent.

    b) A jar of manna, Aaron's staff that had budded, and the stone tablets of the covenant.

    c) A copy of the Psalms, a piece of Moses' staff, and a vial of anointing oil.

3. Who took over leading the Israelites after Moses died?

    a) Aaron

    b) Joshua

    c) Caleb

    d) Miriam

4. What river did the Israelites have to cross to get into the Promised Land?

    a) The Nile River

    b) The Amazon River

    c) The Jordan River

    d) The Imperial River

5. What was the first big city the Israelites had to face in the Promised Land?

    a) Jerusalem

    b) Jericho

    c) Bethlehem

    d) Nazareth

True or False:

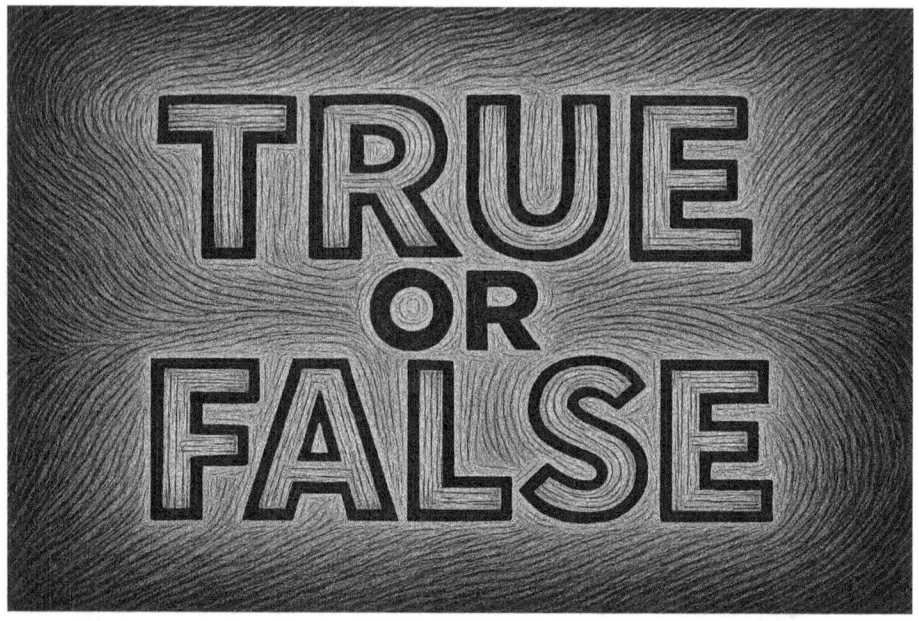

6. True or False: The Israelites were always happy and never complained during their time in the desert.

7. True or False: Moses led the Israelites all the way into the Promised Land.

8. True or False: God gave the Israelites water in the desert by telling Moses to hit a rock with his staff.

9. True or False: The Israelites easily took over the Promised Land without any fighting.

10. True or False: Acacia wood was used to construct the Ark of the Covenant.

Fill in the Blank:

11. The Israelites wandered in the desert for about _____ years.

12. Out of all the spies sent into the Promised Land, only _____ and Caleb said they could take the land.

13. The walls of Jericho fell down after the Israelites marched around the city and the _____ blew their horns.

14. The Promised Land was also called _____.

15. The first book in the Bible after Deuteronomy is _____.

Who Said That?

16. "The land we explored is really, really good!" Who said this?

    a) All the spies

    b) Joshua and Caleb

    c) Moses

    d) Aaron

17. "Just as the Lord commanded his servant Moses, so Moses commanded Joshua, and Joshua did it; he left nothing undone of all that the Lord commanded Moses." What does this tell us about Joshua?

    a) He was a great warrior.

    b) He followed God's instructions completely.

    c) He was really popular with the people.

Bible Book Breakdown:

18. Moses took Joshua to stand before _____ and the entire assembly.

19. The seven day long Holy Festival held on the 15th day of the seventh month was called _____.

Answers

Multiple Choice Missions

1. b) Manna

2. b) A jar of manna, Aaron's staff that had budded, and the stone tablets of the covenant.

3. b) Joshua

4. c) The Jordan River

5. b) Jericho

True or False

6. False

7. False

8. True

9. False

10. True

Fill in the Blank

11. Forty

12. Joshua

13. Priests

14. Canaan

15. Joshua

Who Said That?

16. b) Joshua and Caleb

17. b) He followed God's instructions completely.

Bible Book Breakdown

18. Eleazar the priest

19. The Festival of Tabernacles

Part 6: Kings, Prophets, and Exile - The Ups and Downs of a Nation

After finally settling into the Promised Land, the Israelites' journey was far from simple. Their story unfolds with incredible highs and devastating lows. Get ready for powerful kings, bold prophets who delivered God's messages, and what awaited the Israelites.

Multiple Choice Missions:

1. Who was the first king of Israel?

    a) David

    b) Solomon

    c) Saul

    d) Samuel

2. Which king of Israel was known for being wise and built the temple in Jerusalem?

    a) Ahab

    b) Hezekiah

    c) Solomon

    d) Josiah

3. What was the job of the prophets in ancient Israel?

    a) To predict the weather.

    b) To entertain the king with stories.

    c) To share God's messages with the people and leaders.

4. Which big empire conquered the northern part of Israel and took its people away?

    a) Egypt

    b) Assyria

    c) Babylon

5. Which prophet had a famous vision of a valley full of dry bones coming back to life, showing that Israel could be restored?

    a) Isaiah

    b) Jeremiah

    c) Ezekiel

    d) Daniel

True or False:

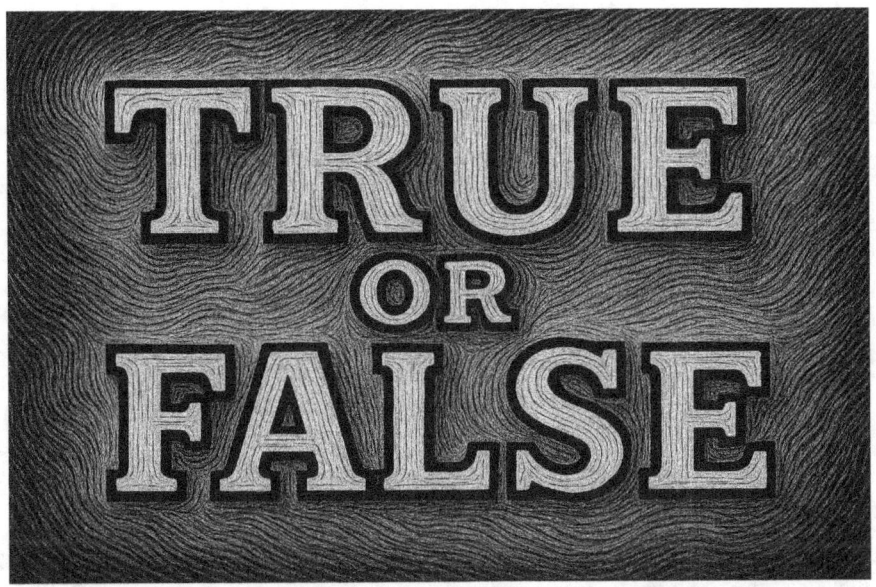

6. True or False: All the kings of Israel and Judah were faithful to God.

7. True or False: The prophet Elijah had a big showdown with false prophets on Mount Carmel.

8. True or False: The southern part of Israel, called Judah, was never taken away into exile.

9. True or False: The prophet Daniel explained dreams for the Babylonian king Nebuchadnezzar.

10. True or False: The Old Testament ends with the Israelites living happily ever after in their own land.

Fill in the Blank:

11. David wrote many of the _____ in the Bible.

12. The northern kingdom of Israel had _____ tribes.

13. The prophet Isaiah talked a lot about the coming _____.

14. The time when the Israelites were forced to live in Babylon lasted for about _____ years.

15. The very last book of the Old Testament is _____.

Who Said That?

16. "Choose for yourselves this day whom you will serve... But as for me and my household, we will serve the Lord." Who said this?

    a) King David

    b) Prophet Elijah

    c) Joshua

17. "The Lord is my shepherd; I shall not want." These famous words are from which book and who wrote them?

    a) Proverbs, King Solomon

    b) Psalms, King David

    c) Isaiah, the Prophet

Bible Book Breakdown:

18. The books that tell the history of Israel's kings and prophets include 1 and 2 Samuel, 1 and 2 Kings, and 1 and 2 _____.

19. The major books written by prophets in the Old Testament include Isaiah, Jeremiah, Ezekiel, and _____.

Answers

Multiple Choice Missions

1. c) Saul
2. c) Solomon
3. c) To share God's messages with the people and leaders.
4. b) Assyria
5. c) Ezekiel

True or False

6. False
7. True
8. False
9. True
10. False

Fill in the Blank

11. Psalms
12. Ten
13. Messiah
14. Seventy
15. Malachi

Who Said That?

16. c) Joshua
17. b) Psalms, King David

Bible Book Breakdown

18. Chronicles
19. Daniel

Part 7: Jesus and the Gospels - The Main Event Begins!

Everything in the Old Testament was leading up to this: Meeting Jesus, the Son of God, whose life, teachings, death, and coming back to life are the most important parts of the Bible. This section focuses on the first four books of the New Testament.

Multiple Choice Missions:

1. In what town was Jesus born?

   a) Jerusalem

   b) Bethlehem

   c) Nazareth

   d) Capernaum

2. Who baptized Jesus in the Jordan River?

   a) Peter

   b) John the Baptist

   c) Mary Magdalene

3. How many main followers (disciples) did Jesus choose?

   a) 7

   b) 12

   c) 20

4. What was the main message Jesus taught?

   a) How to get rich

   b) Following all the rules perfectly

   c) Loving God and loving others

5. What are the stories Jesus often used to teach spiritual lessons called?

   a) Legends

   b) Myths

   c) Parables

True or False:

6. True or False: Jesus did many amazing miracles that showed God's power.

7. True or False: Everyone Jesus met liked and respected him.

8. True or False: Jesus taught his followers the "Our Father" prayer.

9. True or False: Jesus died on a cross, was entombed, and then came back to life three days later.

10. True or False: All four books about Jesus tell the exact same story with no differences.

Fill in the Blank:

11. The first four books of the New Testament are Matthew, Mark, _____, and John.

12. Jesus often called himself the _____ of Man.

13. The last meal Jesus shared with his disciples before he died is called the Last _____.

14. The Roman governor who sentenced Jesus to death was Pontius _____.

15. Christians celebrate Jesus coming back to life on _____.

Who Said That?

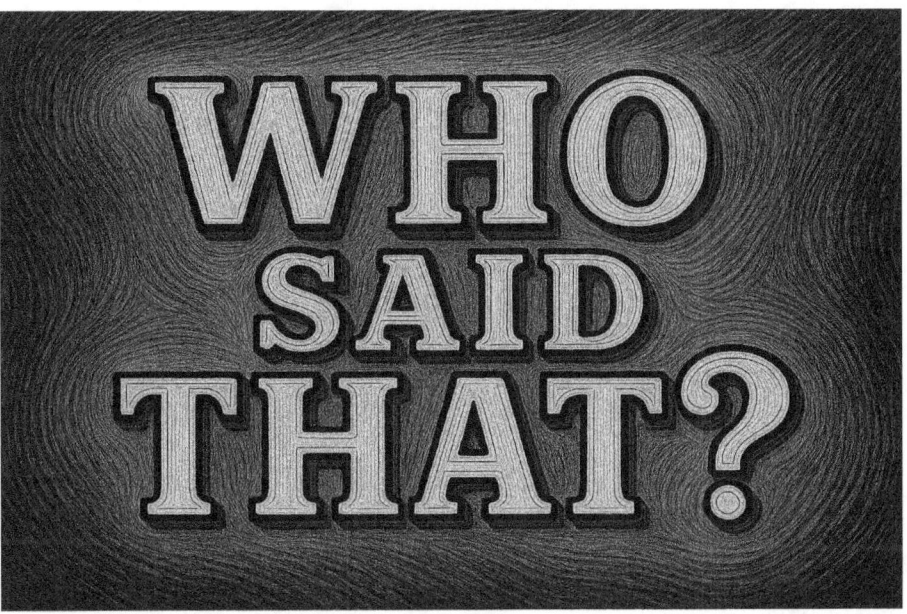

16. "You are the Christ, the Son of the living God." Who said this about Jesus?

    a) Judas Iscariot

    b) Peter

    c) Mary, Jesus' mother

17. "For God so loved the world that he gave his one and only Son, that whoever believes in him shall not perish but have eternal life." This famous verse is in which book?

    a) Matthew

    b) Mark

    c) John

Bible Book Breakdown:

18. The book about Jesus that is often thought to be written for Jewish people, showing him as the Messiah, is _____.

19. The book about Jesus that is known for being fast-paced and focusing on his actions is _____.

Answers

Multiple Choice Missions

1. b) Bethlehem

2. b) John the Baptist

3. b) 12

4. c) Loving God and loving others

5. c) Parables

True or False Trials

6. True

7. False

8. True

9. True

10. False

Fill in the Blank

11. Luke

12. Son

13. Supper

14. Pilate

15. Easter

Who Said That?

16. b) Peter

17. c) John

Bible Book Breakdown

18. Matthew

19. Mark

Part 8: The Early Church and Revelation - The Story Continues

Jesus went back to Heaven, but his followers, filled with God's Spirit, kept doing His work. Get ready for the start of the church, journeys to spread the word, letters of encouragement and correction, and a look into the future in the book of Revelation.

Multiple Choice Missions:

1. What big event happened on the Day of Pentecost?

    a) Jesus went back to Heaven.

    b) The Holy Spirit came upon Jesus' followers.

    c) The first church building was opened.

2. Who was a key leader in the early church who traveled around telling people about Jesus?

    a) Peter

    b) Paul

    c) James

3. What were the letters written by Paul and other leaders mostly about?

    a) Fables.

    b) Telling travel stories.

    c) Encouraging and teaching the first Christians.

4. What is the very last book of the Bible?

    a) Acts

    b) Romans

    c) Revelation

5. What is the book of Revelation mainly about?

    a) Biographies of all the apostles.

    b) How to build churches.

    c) Symbolic visions about the end of the world and God winning in the end.

True or False:

6. True or False: The first Christians had no problems or mean people bothering them.
7. True or False: Paul used to be against Christians before he became one himself.
8. True or False: The book of Acts mostly talks about how the church grew in Jerusalem.
9. True or False: The book of Revelation should be taken as a literal, step-by-step prediction of the future by everyone.
10. True or False: The Bible ends with a hopeful message about God's lasting rule.

Fill in the Blank:

11. The disciple who gave the first big speech on the Day of Pentecost was _____.
12. Paul's big change of heart happened on the road to _____.
13. The city where the first big meeting of church leaders happened to talk about non-Jewish believers was _____.
14. The person who wrote the book of Revelation is usually thought to be the apostle _____.
15. The New Testament ends with a promise of Jesus coming back and God creating a new _____ and a new earth.

Who Said That?

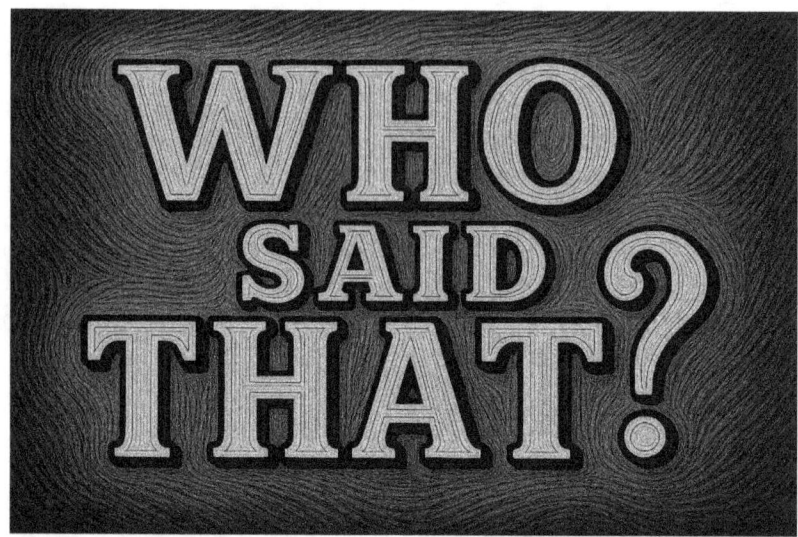

16. "Repent and be baptized, every one of you, in the name of Jesus Christ for the forgiveness of your sins. And you will receive the gift of the Holy Spirit." Who said this?

    a) Paul

    b) Peter

17. "I have fought the good fight, I have finished the race, I have kept the faith." These are thought to be the last words of which apostle before he died?

    a) Peter

    b) Paul

Bible Book Breakdown:

18. The book that tells the story of what happened after Jesus went back to heaven and the church started is _____.

19. The letters written by Paul are called _____.

Answers

Multiple Choice Missions

1. b) The Holy Spirit came upon Jesus' followers.

2. b) Paul

3. c) Encouraging and teaching the first Christians.

4. c) Revelation

5. c) Symbolic visions about the end of the world and God winning in the end.

True or False

6. False

7. True

8. False

9. False

10. True

Fill in the Blank

11. Peter

12. Damascus

13. Antioch

14. John

15. Heaven

Who Said That?

16. b) Peter

17. b) Paul

Bible Book Breakdown

18. Acts

19. Epistles

Section 2: Awesome People of the Bible

Part 1: The Faith Hall of Famers (Old Testament Heroes)

The Old Testament has several incredible stories of people who trusted God in amazing ways, even when things got tough. These "Faith Hall of Famers" faced huge challenges, made some mistakes, but their stories teach us a lot about what it means to follow God.

Multiple Choice Missions:

1. What was away Abraham showed his trust in God?

    a) By always having the best sacrifices.

    b) By immediately obeying God's call to leave his homeland.

    c) By arguing with God whenever he disagreed.

    d) By becoming the richest person in his region.

2. Moses led the Israelites out of Egypt. What was his initial reaction when God asked him to do this?

    a) He was excited and ready to go.

    b) He felt unqualified and made excuses.

    c) He asked for a sign to prove God was real.

    d) He immediately went to Pharaoh.

3. King David wasn't just a king; he was also known for something else he did. What was it?

    a) He was a great architect.

    b) He was a skilled musician and songwriter (many of the Psalms!).

    c) He was a famous inventor.

    d) He was a powerful military general from a young age.

4. Ruth was a Moabite woman who showed incredible loyalty. To whom was she fiercely loyal?

    a) Her former gods.

    b) The king of Moab.

    c) Her mother-in-law, Naomi.

    d) The other women in her village.

5. Esther became queen of Persia. What brave thing did she do to help her people?

    a) She started a rebellion against the king.

    b) She hid her identity and risked her life to speak to the king.

    c) She used her wealth to bribe the king's officials.

    d) She escaped and warned her people from afar.

True or False:

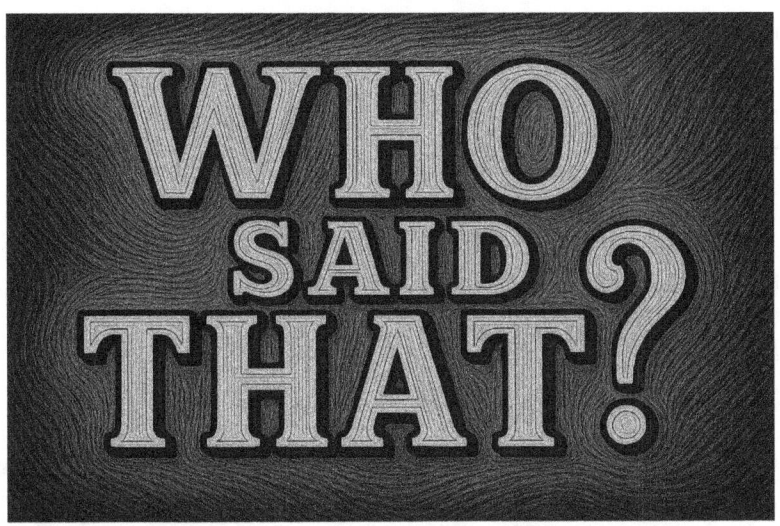

6. True or False: Abraham never doubted God's promises.

7. True or False: Moses was a confident and skilled public speaker from the beginning of his mission.

8. True or False: David never made any mistakes or sinned during his reign as king.

9. True or False: Ruth chose to return to her homeland after her husband died.

10. True or False: Esther's uncle Mordecai encouraged her to hide her Jewish identity.

Fill in the Blank:

11. God promised Abraham that his descendants would be as numerous as the _____ in the sky.

12. Moses performed many miracles using the _____ that God gave him.

13. David famously defeated the giant _____ with a slingshot and stones.

14. Ruth's famous declaration of loyalty to Naomi included the words, "Your people will be my people, and your _____ my _____."

15. Esther's courage led to the celebration of the Jewish festival of _____.

Who Am I?

16. I was willing to sacrifice my beloved son because God asked me to. My faith was tested in a big way. Who am I?

    a) Moses

    b) Abraham

    c) David

    d) Noah

17. I led my people out of slavery, but I wasn't allowed to enter the Promised Land myself. Who am I?

    a) Joshua

    b) Moses

    c) Abraham

    d) Joseph

Bible Book Breakdown:

18. The story of Abraham's early life and God's covenant with him is mainly found in the book of _____.

19. The story of Ruth and her loyalty is told in the book of _____.

Answers

Multiple Choice Missions

1. b) By immediately obeying God's call to leave his homeland.

2. b) He felt unqualified and made excuses.

3. b) He was a skilled musician and songwriter (many of the Psalms!).

4. c) Her mother-in-law, Naomi.

5. b) She hid her identity and risked her life to speak to the king.

True or False

6. False

7. False

8. False

9. False

10. False

Fill in the Blank

11. stars

12. staff

13. Goliath

14. God, God

15. Purim

Who Said That?

16. b) Abraham

17. b) Moses

Bible Book Breakdown

18. Genesis

19. Ruth

Part 2: Jesus' Inner Circle - The Twelve Disciples

Jesus chose 12 disciples that walked with him, learned from him, and were sent out to share his message. These disciples came from different walks of life, and their stories are part of the Biblical history that we know today.

Multiple Choice Missions:

1. Which of Jesus' disciples was a fisherman and often considered the leader of the group?

   a) John

   b) Peter

   c) James

   d) Andrew

2. Which disciple was a tax collector before following Jesus?

   a) Simon the Zealot

   b) Matthew

   c) Philip

   d) Thomas

3. Which two disciples were brothers and known for their fiery personalities (Jesus even nicknamed them "Sons of Thunder")?

   a) Peter and Andrew

   b) James and John

   c) Philip and Bartholomew

   d) Thaddeus and Simon

4. Which disciple is famous for doubting Jesus' resurrection until he saw him with his own eyes?

   a) James

   b) Thomas

   c) Matthew

   d) Judas

5. Which disciple betrayed Jesus for thirty pieces of silver?

   a) Peter

   b) John

   c) Judas Iscariot

   d) Philip

True or False:

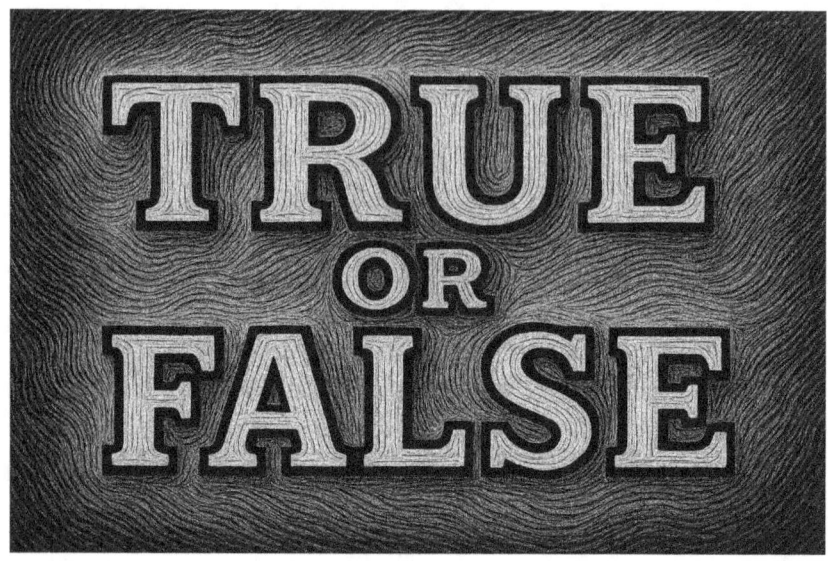

6. True or False: All twelve disciples were quick to understand Jesus' teachings.

7. True or False: Peter walked on water just like Jesus did.

8. True or False: John was known as "the disciple whom Jesus loved."

9. True or False: Matthew kept his tax collector job while following Jesus.

10. True or False: After Jesus' ascension, all twelve disciples remained in Jerusalem.

Fill in the Blank:

11. Peter's original name was _____.

12. Andrew was Peter's _____.

13. James and John were the sons of _____.

14. Philip brought his friend _____ to meet Jesus.

15. Thomas said he wouldn't believe Jesus had risen unless he saw the nail marks in his _____ and put his finger where the nails had been.

Who Am I?

16. I denied knowing Jesus three times, even though I had promised to follow him anywhere. Who am I?

    a) John

    b) Peter

    c) James

    d) Thomas

17. I was in charge of the money bag for the disciples and sometimes helped myself to it. Who am I?

    a) Matthew

    b) Philip

    c) Judas Iscariot

    d) Simon the Zealot

Bible Book Breakdown:

18. The stories of Jesus calling his disciples and their early ministry are found in the Gospels of Matthew, Mark, _____, and John.

19. The book of _____ tells about what the disciples did after Jesus ascended to heaven.

Answers

Multiple Choice Missions

1. b) Peter

2. b) Matthew

3. b) James and John

4. b) Thomas

5. c) Judas Iscariot

True or False

6. False

7. True

8. True

9. False

10. False

Fill in the Blank

11. Simon

12. brother

13. Zebedee

14. Nathanael

15. hands

Who Said That?

16. b) Peter

17. c) Judas Iscariot

Bible Book Breakdown

18. Luke

19. Acts

Part 3: Game Changers - Other Influential People

The Bible isn't just about the big heroes and the 12 disciples. There are others who played important roles in God's story. This part highlights some of these "Game Changers": people who, in their own way, significantly impacted the narrative of faith.

Multiple Choice Missions:

1. Mary Magdalene was one of Jesus' devoted followers. What special privilege did she have after his resurrection?

    a) She performed the first miracle after Jesus rose.

    b) She was the first person Jesus appeared to after rising from the dead.

    c) She became the leader of the early church.

    d) She wrote one of the Gospels.

2. Paul (originally Saul) was a major figure in the early church. What was he doing before he became a follower of Jesus?

    a) He was a Roman soldier.

    b) He was a fisherman alongside Peter.

    c) He was actively persecuting Christians.

    d) He was a tax collector.

3. Deborah was a unique leader in the Old Testament. What role did she primarily serve?

    a) She was a queen.

    b) She was a prophet and a judge.

    c) She was a military commander.

    d) She was a musician in the temple.

4. Elijah was a powerful prophet in the Old Testament. What dramatic event marked the end of his earthly ministry?

    a) He was stoned by his enemies.

    b) He died of old age surrounded by his followers.

    c) He was taken up to heaven in a whirlwind.

    d) He was thrown into a lions' den.

5. Timothy was a young man who became a close companion and helper of which apostle?

    a) Peter

    b) John

    c) Paul

    d) James

True or False:

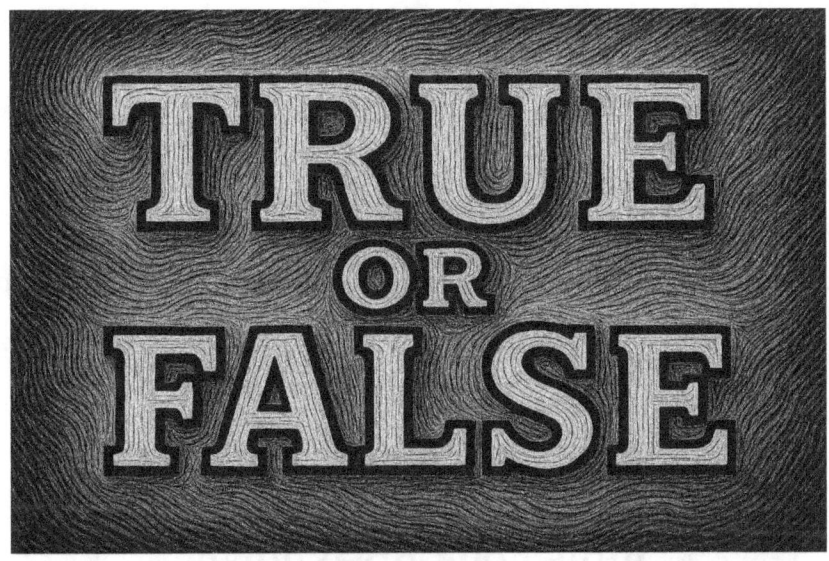

6. True or False: Mary, the mother of Jesus, played no significant role in his ministry after his birth.

7. True or False: Paul was never imprisoned for his faith.

8. True or False: Deborah personally led the Israelite army into battle.

9. True or False: Elijah performed many miracles, including raising someone from the dead.

10. True or False: Timothy was older than Paul.

Fill in the Blank:

11. Mary Magdalene was among the women who first visited Jesus' _____ after his crucifixion.

12. Paul wrote many _____ that are now part of the New Testament.

13. Deborah prophesied that the commander Barak would only achieve victory if she went with him into _____.

14. Elijah challenged the prophets of _____ to a contest on Mount Carmel.

15. Paul wrote two letters specifically addressed to _____, giving him guidance for church leadership.

Who Am I?

16. I was a woman who supported Jesus' ministry financially and was present at his crucifixion and resurrection. Who am I?

    a) Mary, the mother of Jesus

    b) Martha

    c) Mary Magdalene

    d) Salome

17. I was a powerful speaker and a key figure in the early church in Alexandria, known for my eloquent teaching. Who am I?

    a) Barnabas

    b) Apollos

    c) Silas

    d) Luke

Bible Book Breakdown:

18. The stories of Mary Magdalene's encounters with the risen Jesus are found in all four _____.

19. Many of Paul's letters, including those to Timothy, are found in the _____ Testament.

Answers

Multiple Choice Missions

1. b) She was the first person Jesus appeared to after rising from the dead.

2. c) He was actively persecuting Christians.

3. b) She was a prophet and a judge.

4. c) He was taken up to heaven in a whirlwind.

5. c) Paul

True or False

6. False

7. False

8. False

9. True

10. False

Fill in the Blank

11. tomb

12. letters

13. Mount Tabor

14. Baal

15. Timothy

Who Said That?

16. c) Mary Magdalene

17. b) Apollos

Bible Book Breakdown

18. Gospels

19. New

Part 4: Tricky Tales - Complex or Controversial Figures

The Bible doesn't shy away from flawed individuals and complex stories. This part looks at people whose lives raise tough questions or whose actions were a mix of good and bad. Exploring these figures helps us understand that faith isn't always simple and that God can work through imperfect people.

Multiple Choice Missions:

1. Samson was known for his incredible strength. What was the source of his power?

   a) Special armor he wore.

   b) A magic potion he drank.

   c) His uncut hair, as part of a vow to God.

   d) His intense physical training.

2. Jonah was a prophet who disobeyed God's command. What was he told to do?

   a) To go and preach to the city of Jerusalem.

   b) To go and preach to the city of Nineveh.

   c) To go and preach to the Israelites in exile.

   d) To go and preach to the Pharaoh of Egypt.

3. King Solomon was known for his wisdom, but he also made some questionable choices. What was one of his major downfalls?

   a) He lost all his wealth.

   b) He angered God by marrying many foreign women and allowing the worship of their gods.

   c) He became a cruel and unjust ruler.

   d) He stopped believing in God.

4. Saul was the first king of Israel. Why did God eventually reject him as king?

   a) He was too kind to his enemies.

   b) He disobeyed God's direct commands.

   c) He wasn't a good military leader.

   d) He tried to make himself a prophet.

5. Judas Iscariot's motives for betraying Jesus are debated. What is one possible reason mentioned in the Bible?

   a) He hated Jesus' teachings.

   b) He was promised a large sum of money.

   c) He wanted to force Jesus to start a rebellion.

   d) All of the above.

True or False:

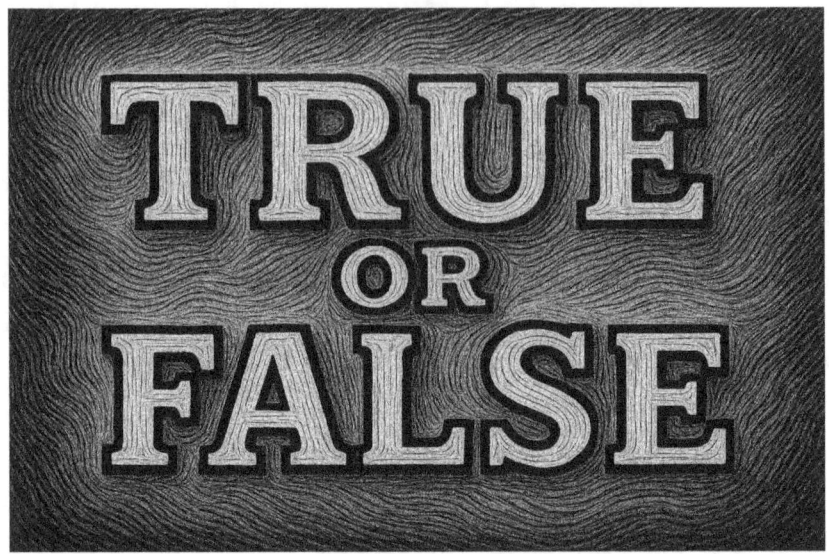

6. True or False: Samson always used his strength for good.

7. True or False: Jonah was happy to go to Nineveh after he was rescued from the big fish.

8. True or False: Solomon remained faithful to God throughout his entire life.

9. True or False: Saul humbly accepted God's decision to replace him as king.

10. True or False: The Bible clearly states that Judas betrayed Jesus solely for the money.

Fill in the Blank:

11. Samson was ultimately betrayed by _____ who cut his hair.

12. Jonah was swallowed by a _____ when he tried to run away from God.

13. Solomon's wisdom is highlighted in the story of how he settled a dispute between two _____.

14. Saul tried to kill _____ out of jealousy.

15. After betraying Jesus, Judas felt great remorse and _____ himself.

Who Am I?

16. I was incredibly strong, but my weakness for a woman led to my downfall. Who am I?

   a) Solomon

   b) Samson

   c) Saul

   d) Jonah

17. I was a king known for my wisdom, but I also allowed idol worship in Israel. Who am I?

   a) David

   b) Solomon

   c) Hezekiah

   d) Josiah

Bible Book Breakdown:

18. The story of Samson and his strength is found in the book of _____.

19. The story of Jonah and the big fish is told in the book of _____.

Answers

Multiple Choice Missions

1. c) His uncut hair, as part of a vow to God.

2. b) To go and preach to the city of Nineveh.

3. b) He angered God by marrying many foreign women and allowing the worship of their gods.

4. b) He disobeyed God's direct commands.

5. b) He was promised a large sum of money.

True or False

6. False

7. False

8. False

9. False

10. False

Fill in the Blank:

11. Delilah

12. large fish

13. prostitutes

14. David

15. hanged

Who Said That?

16. b) Samson

17. b) Solomon

Bible Book Breakdown

18. Judges

19. Jonah

Section 3: Theme Park - Exploring Key Biblical Themes

Part 1: Love & Relationships (God's love, friendship, family)

This section explores crucial connections: from the unconditional love God has for us, to the rock-solid bonds of true friendship, and even the seriously complicated dynamics within families. Get ready to gain a fresh perspective on how to navigate your own connections.

Multiple Choice Missions:

1. The Bible often describes God's love for humanity using what powerful comparison?

    a) Like a strict teacher for their students.

    b) Like a distant king for their subjects.

    c) Like a loving parent for their child.

    d) Like a ship captain to a crew.

2. Who in the Old Testament is known for their incredibly close and loyal friendship?

    a) Abraham and Lot

    b) Moses and Aaron

    c) David and Jonathan

    d) Jacob and Esau

3. The story of the prodigal son is a powerful illustration of what aspect of God's love?

    a) His preference for those who always obey.

    b) His anger towards those who mess up.

    c) His forgiving and welcoming nature.

    d) His desire for perfect people.

4. What is often referred to as the "greatest commandment" by Jesus?

    a) To always attend religious services.

    b) To follow all the rules perfectly.

    c) To love God with all your heart and to love your neighbor as yourself.

    d) To give all your money to the poor.

5. The Bible emphasizes the importance of unity and love within the Christian community. What analogy does it sometimes use to describe this?

    a) Like individual trees in a forest.

    b) Like different instruments in an orchestra.

    c) Like separate islands in an ocean.

    d) Like scattered stones on a beach.

True or False:

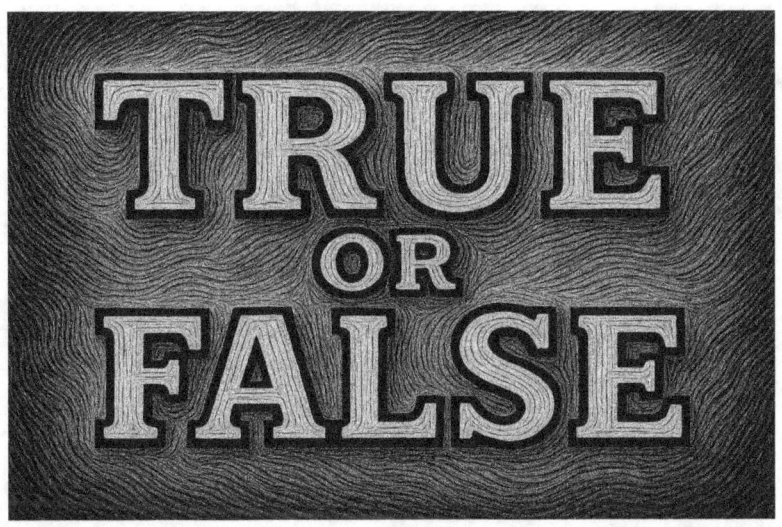

6. True or False: God's love is conditional; we have to earn it by being good.

7. True or False: The friendship between David and Jonathan faced no challenges.

8. True or False: In the story of the prodigal son, the older brother was very happy about his younger brother's return.

9. True or False: Jesus taught that loving your enemies is impossible.

10. True or False: The Bible encourages believers to isolate themselves from non-believers to maintain their purity.

Fill in the Blank:

11. "For God so _____ the world that he gave his one and only Son..." (John 3:16)

12. Jonathan showed his love for David by giving him his robe, his tunic, his sword, his bow, and his _____.

13. When the prodigal son returned home, his father _____ him and kissed him.

14. Jesus said, "A new command I give you: Love one another. As I have loved you, so you must _____ one another." (John 13:34)

15. "Be completely humble and gentle; be patient, bearing with one another in _____." (Ephesians 4:2)

Who Said That?

16. "Where you go I will go, and where you stay I will stay. Your people will be my people and your God my God." Who said this as an expression of deep loyalty and love?

    a) Ruth to Naomi

    b) David to Jonathan

    c) The prodigal son to his father

    d) Esther to Mordecai

17. "Greater love has no one than this: to lay down one's life for one's friends." Who said this?

    a) Paul

    b) Peter

    c) Jesus

    d) John

Bible Book Breakdown:

18. The story of the deep friendship between David and Jonathan is primarily found in the book of _____.

19. Jesus' teachings about love are central to all four _____.

Answers

Multiple Choice Missions

1. c) Like a loving parent for their child.

2. c) David and Jonathan

3. c) His forgiving and welcoming nature.

4. c) To love God with all your heart and to love your neighbor as yourself.

5. b) Like different instruments in an orchestra.

True or False

6. False

7. False

8. False

9. False

10. False

Fill in the Blank

11. loved

12. robe

13. hugged/embraced

14. love

15. patience

Who Said That?

16. a) Ruth to Naomi

17. c) Jesus

Bible Book Breakdown:

18. 1 Samuel/2 Samuel

19. Gospels

Part 2: Forgiveness & Redemption (Second chances, grace)

The Bible has powerful stories of second chances and how God offers forgiveness and redemption, even when people mess up big time. This section explores this important theme.

Multiple Choice Missions:

1. After denying Jesus three times, which disciple was eventually restored and became a key leader in the early church?

    a) Judas Iscariot

    b) Thomas

    c) Peter

    d) John

2. The story of the woman caught in adultery, whom the religious leaders wanted to stone, highlights what aspect of Jesus' character?

    a) His strict adherence to the law.

    b) His fear of public opinion.

    c) His compassion and offer of forgiveness.

3. The parable of the lost sheep illustrates God's attitude towards those who wander away. What does the shepherd do when he realizes a sheep is missing?

    a) He blames the lost sheep.

    b) He ignores the lost sheep and focuses on the others.

    c) He leaves the ninety-nine to search for the one lost sheep.

    d) He punishes the other sheep for not keeping watch.

4. Paul, who wrote many books in the New Testament, had a past of doing what to Christians before his conversion?

    a) Praising them publicly.

    b) Ignoring them completely.

    c) Actively persecuting and imprisoning them.

    d) Secretly helping them.

5. The concept of "grace" in the Bible refers to what?

    a) Earning God's favor through good deeds.

    b) God's unearned and undeserved favor.

    c) God's obligation to forgive everyone.

    d) God only helping perfect people.

True or False:

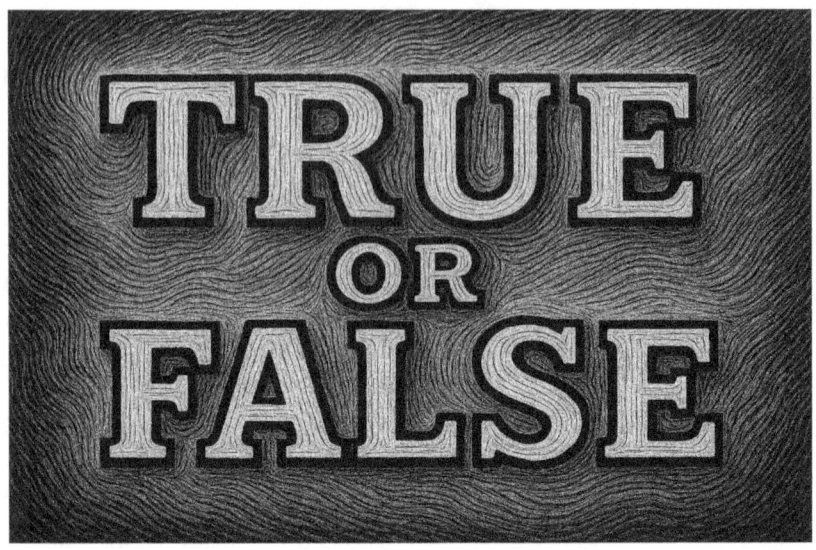

6. True or False: Peter never fully recovered from the shame of denying Jesus.

7. True or False: Jesus told the woman caught in adultery that her sin was acceptable.

8. True or False: The parable of the lost sheep emphasizes the value God places on each individual.

9. True or False: Paul's past actions were held against him by the other apostles and early Christians.

10. True or False: Grace means God overlooks our sins without any consequences.

Fill in the Blank:

11. When Peter denied Jesus, a _____ crowed.

12. Jesus told the woman caught in adultery, "Go now and leave your life of _____." (John 8:11)

13. In the parable of the lost sheep, there is more rejoicing in heaven over one sinner who _____ than over ninety-nine righteous persons who do not need to repent. (Luke 15:7)

14. Paul's _____ happened on the road to Damascus

15. "For it is by _____ you have been saved, through faith—and this is not from yourselves, it is the gift of God." (Ephesians 2:8)

Who Said That?

16. "Father, forgive them, for they do not know what they are doing." Who said this while being crucified?

    a) Peter

    b) Paul

    c) Jesus

    d) One of the criminals crucified with Jesus

17. "Even though I was once a blasphemer and a persecutor and a violent man, I was shown mercy because I acted in ignorance and unbelief." Who wrote these words reflecting on their past?

    a) Peter

    b) Paul

    c) John

    d) James

Bible Book Breakdown:

18. The story of Peter's denial and restoration is found in all four _____.

19. Paul's conversion and his teachings on grace are prominent in his letters, especially the book of _____.

Answers

Multiple Choice Missions

1. c) Peter
2. c) His compassion and offer of forgiveness.
3. c) He leaves the ninety-nine to search for the one lost sheep.
4. c) Actively persecuting and imprisoning them.
5. b) God's unearned and undeserved favor.

True or False

6. False
7. False
8. True
9. False
10. False

Fill in the Blank

11. rooster/cock
12. sin
13. repents
14. conversion
15. grace

Who Said That?

16. c) Jesus
17. b) Paul

Bible Book Breakdown

18. Gospels
19. Romans

Part 3: Faith & Trust (Believing in God, even when it's hard)

Throughout the Bible, we see examples of people who had strong faith and trusted God, even in difficult or seemingly impossible situations. This section explores what it means to have faith and trust in God.

Multiple Choice Missions:

1. Abraham is a prime example of faith. What specific act is often highlighted as his ultimate test of trust in God?

    a) Building an altar to God.

    b) Leaving his homeland.

    c) Being willing to sacrifice his son Isaac.

    d) Arguing with God about Sodom and Gomorrah.

2. When the Israelites were trapped between the Egyptian army and the Red Sea, what did Moses tell them to do?

    a) Surrender to the Egyptians.

    b) Try to swim across the sea.

    c) Stand firm and see the deliverance the Lord would bring.

    d) Build boats to escape.

3. Daniel showed great faith by continuing to pray to God even when it was against the king's decree. What was the consequence of his faith?

    a) He was promoted to a higher position.

    b) He was thrown into a fiery furnace.

    c) He was thrown into a lions' den.

    d) He was exiled from the kingdom.

4. Jesus often told his followers that their faith had healed them. What does this suggest about the role of faith in experiencing God's power?

    a) Faith forces God to act.

    b) God only helps those with perfect faith.

    c) Faith is often a key element in receiving what God offers.

    d) God acts regardless of whether people believe.

5. The book of Hebrews talks about faith as being sure of what we hope for and certain of what we do not see. What does this imply about faith?

    a) It's based on visible evidence.

    b) It requires understanding everything perfectly.

    c) It involves believing in things that aren't yet tangible.

    d) It's the same as wishful thinking.

True or False:

6. True or False: Abraham fully understood God's plan for his descendants when he was first called.

7. True or False: The Israelites were always confident and trusting in God during their wilderness journey.

8. True or False: Daniel's faith protected him from any harm in the lions' den.

9. True or False: Jesus only healed people who had a lot of religious knowledge.

10. True or False: The Bible teaches that doubt and faith cannot coexist.

Fill in the Blank:

11. By _____ Abraham obeyed when God called him to go to a place he would later receive as his inheritance. (Hebrews 11:8)

12. When Moses stretched out his hand over the Red Sea, the Lord drove the sea back with a strong _____ wind and turned it into dry land. (Exodus 14:21)

13. Daniel continued to get down on his knees three times a day to pray and give thanks to his God, just as he had done _____. (Daniel 6:10)

14. Jesus often said, "Your _____ has healed you; go in peace." (e.g., Luke 8:48)

15. "Without _____ it is impossible to please God, because anyone who comes to him must believe that he exists and that he rewards those who earnestly seek him." (Hebrews 11:6)

Who Said That?

16. "But without faith it is impossible to please God..." Who wrote these words emphasizing the importance of faith?

   a) Peter

   b) Paul (the author of Hebrews is traditionally attributed to Paul or someone in his circle)

   c) James

   d) John

17. "Lord, I believe; help my unbelief!" Who said this, expressing a struggle between faith and doubt?

   a) Abraham

   b) Moses

   c) The father of a possessed boy

   d) Thomas

Bible Book Breakdown:

18. The story of Abraham's test of faith is primarily found in the book of _____.

19. The book of _____ is often called the "hall of faith" for its examples of those who trusted God.

Answers

Multiple Choice Missions

1. c) Being willing to sacrifice his son Isaac.

2. c) Stand firm and see the deliverance the Lord would bring.

3. c) He was thrown into a lions' den.

4. c) Faith is often a key element in receiving what God offers.

5. c) It involves believing in things that aren't yet tangible.

True or False

6. False

7. False

8. True

9. False

10. False

Fill in the Blank

11. faith

12. east

13. before

14. faith

15. faith

Who Said That?

16. b) Paul (or the author of Hebrews)

17. c) The father of a demon-possessed boy

Bible Book Breakdown

18. Genesis

19. Hebrews

Part 4: Hope & Perseverance

The Bible has several examples of people who faced impossible odds and didn't give up, all because of hope and perseverance. This section is all about how faith helps us push through.

Multiple Choice Missions

1. Which Old-Testament prophet said, "Though a righteous man falls seven times, he rises again"?

   a) Jeremiah

   b) Micah

   c) Isaiah

   d) Solomon

2. When Paul and Silas were thrown into prison, what did they do at midnight?

   a) Slept

   b) Complained

   c) Sang hymns and prayed

   d) Planned an escape

3. Who urged the Israelites, "Be strong and courageous... the LORD himself goes before you"?

   a) Joshua

   b) Moses

   c) Caleb

   d) Samuel

4. Which New-Testament letter pictures hope as "an anchor for the soul"?

   a) James

   b) 1 Peter

   c) Hebrews

   d) Jude

5. The woman who touched Jesus' cloak had been sick for how many years?

   a) 7

   b) 10

   c) 12

   d) 38

True or False:

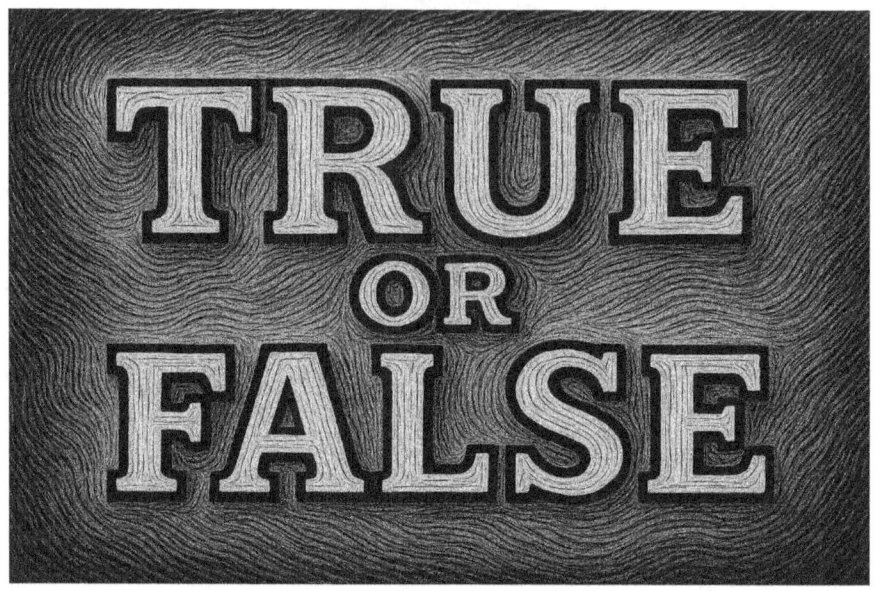

6. True or False: Job's friends immediately comforted him without judging him.
7. True or False: Noah is described as "blameless" in his generation.
8. True or False: Jeremiah quit preaching after being mocked.
9. True or False: Ruth persevered in caring for Naomi even when it meant gleaning leftovers.
10. True or False: Paul compared the Christian life to running a race that requires endurance.

Fill in the Blank:

11. "Those who hope in the LORD will renew their _____."
12. While in the lions' den, the lions' mouths were shut by _____.
13. Jesus told a parable of a persistent _____ who kept asking a judge for justice.
14. In Revelation, the church at Smyrna is encouraged to be faithful even to the point of _____.
15. Hebrews says we are surrounded by a great cloud of _____.

Who Said That?

16. "Even if he slays me, yet will I hope in him."
    a) David
    b) Job
    c) Hezekiah
    d) Habakkuk

17. "I have fought the good fight, I have finished the race, I have kept the faith."
    a) Peter
    b) Paul
    c) John
    d) Stephen

Bible Book Breakdown

18. Habakkuk's dialogue of questions and hope is in the book of
    _____.

19. The prison-worship episode of Paul and Silas appears in the book of _____.

Answers

Multiple Choice Missions

1. d) Solomon

2. c) Sang hymns and prayed

3. a) Joshua

4. c) Hebrews

5. c) 12

True or False

6. False

7. True

8. False

9. True

10. True

Fill in the Blank

11. strength

12. an angel

13. Widow

14. Death

15. Witnesses

Who Said That?

16. b) Job

17. b) Paul

Bible Book Breakdown

18. Habakkuk

19. Acts

Part 5: Prayer & Worship

Have you ever thought about how you connect with the most important people in your life? With God, that connection is profound and transformative. This section explores prayer and worship, and how we express our reverence and adoration for Him.

Multiple Choice Missions:

1. Who wrote the line "Create in me a clean heart, O God"?

    a) Asaph

    b) David

    c) Solomon

    d) Ezra

2. Where was Jesus when the disciples asked, "Lord, teach us to pray"?

    a) Mount of Olives

    b) A synagogue

    c) A certain place, after he had been praying

    d) The Temple

3. Which king played the harp and introduced music teams for temple worship?

    a) Hezekiah

    b) Josiah

    c) David

    d) Jehoshaphat

4. Hannah's heartfelt prayer for a son is in which book?

    a) Ruth

    b) 1 Samuel

    c) Judges

    d) 2 Kings

5. Who thanked God three times a day facing Jerusalem, even under threat of death?

    a) Nehemiah

    b) Daniel

    c) Mordecai

    d) Ezra

True or False:

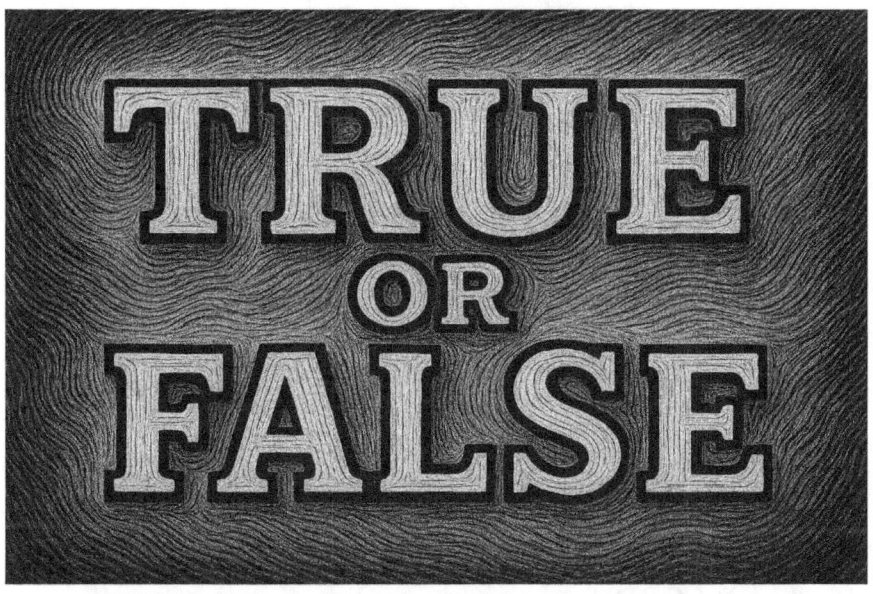

6. True or False: Jesus' "Lord's Prayer" is found only in Matthew.

7. True or False: Paul instructs believers to "pray without ceasing."

8. True or False: Miriam led Israel in worship with a tambourine after crossing the Red Sea.

9. True or False: The Psalms were Israel's primary songbook of worship.

10. True or False: Only priests were allowed to pray in Old-Testament times.

Fill in the Blank:

11. "Enter his gates with _____ and his courts with praise."

12. Jesus said, "True worshipers will worship the Father in spirit and in _____."

13. The early church "devoted themselves to the apostles' teaching and to _____."

14. Paul and Silas were praying in the prison at the city of _____.

15. Psalm 150 ends with "Let everything that has _____ praise the LORD."

Who Said That?

16. "Speak, LORD, for your servant is listening."

   a) Samuel

   b) Solomon

   c) Elisha

   d) Gideon

17. "Bless the LORD, O my soul, and forget not all his benefits."

   a) Moses

   b) David

   c) Isaiah

   d) Jonah

Bible Book Breakdown:

18. Jesus' high-priestly prayer for his disciples is in John chapter _____.

19. Paul's hymn about Christ emptying himself appears in the book of _____ (chapter 2).

Answers

Multiple Choice Missions

1. b) David

2. c) A certain place, after he had been praying

3. c) David

4. b) 1 Samuel

5. b) Daniel

True or False

6. False

7. True

8. True

9. True

10. False

Fill in the Blank

11. Thanksgiving

12. Truth

13. fellowship/prayer

14. Philippi

15. breath

Who Said That?

16. a) Samuel

17. b) David

Bible Breakdown

18. 17

19. Philippian

Part 6: Wisdom & Guidance

God's Word is packed with wisdom to help you navigate life. This section is all about finding that divine direction and making smart moves for your life.

Multiple Choice Missions:

1. Which book personifies Wisdom as a woman calling out in the streets?

   a) Job

   b) Ecclesiastes

   c) Proverbs

   d) Psalms

2. Solomon asked God for what gift when he became king?

   a) Riches

   b) Long life

   c) Wisdom

   d) Military power

3. Which NT epistle says, "If any of you lacks wisdom, you should ask God"?

   a) 1 Peter

   b) James

   c) Hebrews

   d) Jude

4. Who advised Moses to appoint helpers to judge smaller cases?

   a) Aaron

   b) Jethro

   c) Joshua

   d) Caleb

5. The phrase "Fear of the LORD is the beginning of knowledge" appears first in which chapter?

   a) Proverbs 1

   b) Psalm 1

   c) Job 28

   d) Ecclesiastes 12

True or False:

6. True or False: The book of James compares doubting to a wave of the sea blown and tossed by the wind.

7. True or False: Ecclesiastes concludes that everything is meaningless, full stop, with no hope.

8. True or False: Gideon sought guidance by placing a fleece of wool on the ground.

9. True or False: Jesus told a parable about wise and foolish builders to teach about obedience.

10. True or False: Paul relied only on visions for guidance, never on advice from believers.

Fill in the Blank:

11. "Your word is a lamp to my _____ and a light for my path."

12. Proverbs warns, "Trust in the LORD with all your heart and lean not on your own _____."

13. Isaiah promises, "Whether you turn to the right or to the left, you will hear a voice saying, 'This is the _____; walk in it.'"

14. Jesus told Martha that only one thing was needed, and _____ had chosen it.

15. The Urim and _____ were priestly tools used to discern God's will.

Who Said That?

16. "Give your servant a discerning heart to govern your people."

    a) David

    b) Solomon

    c) Hezekiah

    d) Josiah

17. "I will instruct you and teach you in the way you should go."

    a) God in Psalm 32

    b) Moses

    c) Elijah

    d) Paul

Bible Book Breakdown:

18. The famous "fleece test" of Gideon appears in the book of
_____.

19. Proverbs 31's acrostic poem praises a wife of _____
character.

Answers

Multiple Choice Missions

1. c) Proverbs

2. c) Wisdom

3. b) James

4. b) Jethro

5. a) Proverbs 1

True or False

6. True

7. False

8. True

9. True

10. False

Fill in the Blank

11. Feet

12. Understanding

13. Way

14. Mary

15. Thummim

Who Said That?

16. b) Solomon

17. a) God in Psalm 32

Bible Book Breakdown

18. Judges

19. noble/excellent

Part 7: Justice & Mercy

Have you ever been in a situation where something just didn't feel fair? Or maybe you messed up and desperately hoped for a second chance? That's exactly what this section is about: God's heart for justice and His incredible mercy. Let's take a closer look at how God stands for what's right and also how He extends amazing grace.

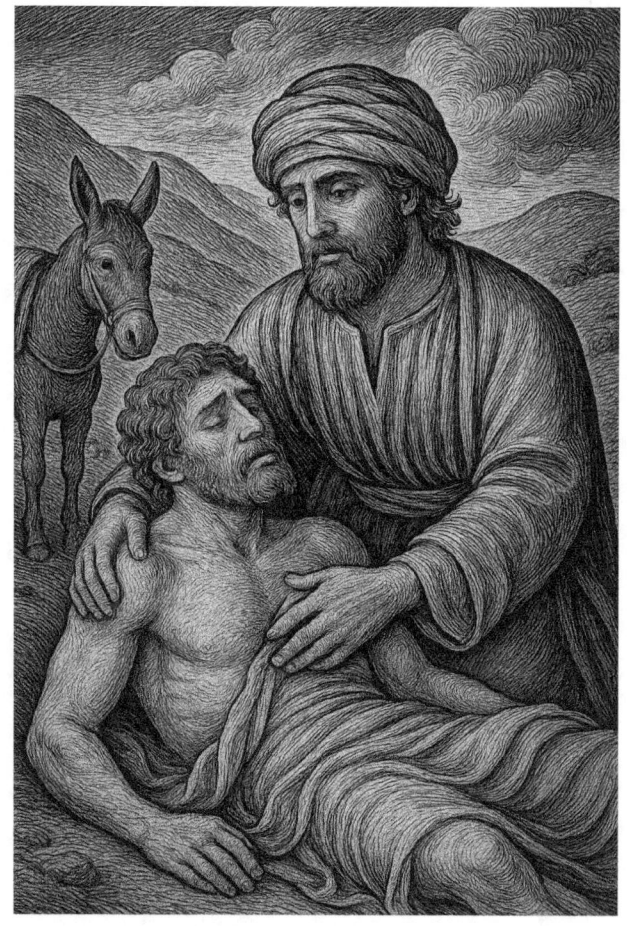

Multiple Choice Missions:

1. Which prophet declared, "Let justice roll on like a river"?

    a) Joel

    b) Amos

    c) Micah

    d) Hosea

2. Jesus illustrated neighbor-love with the parable of the _____ Samaritan.

    a) Caring

    b) Good

    c) Generous

    d) Great

3. Which Old-Testament law ensured the poor could gather leftover crops?

    a) Tithing

    b) Gleaning

    c) Jubilee

    d) Cities of refuge

4. Micah 6:8 says God requires us to act justly, love mercy, and walk _____ with him.

    a) Boldly

    b) Humbly

    c) Quickly

    d) Perfectly

5. Who pleaded for Sodom, asking if God would spare the city for ten righteous people?

    a) Lot

    b) Abraham

    c) Jacob

    d) Isaac

True or False:

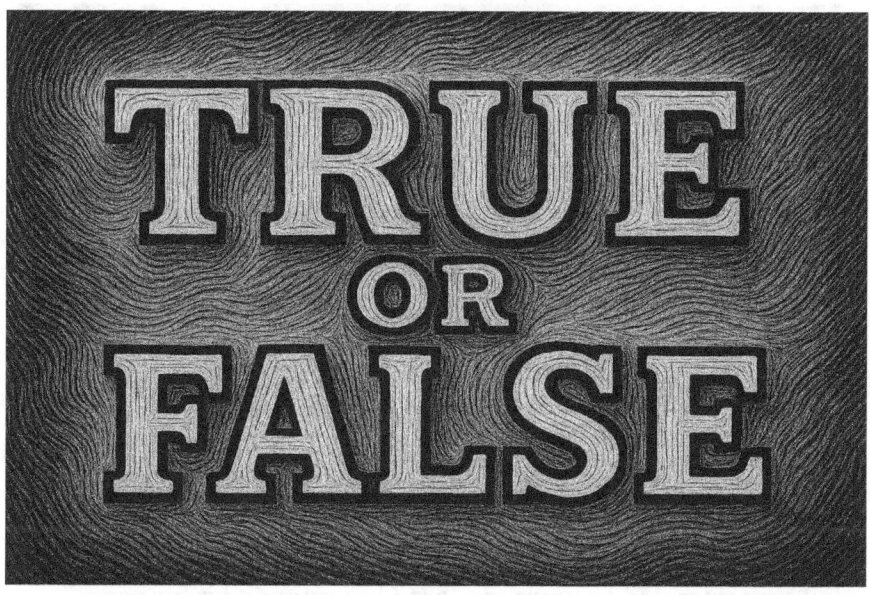

6. True or False: The Year of Jubilee canceled debts and returned land every 50 years.

7. True or False: Jonah was excited when God forgave Nineveh.

8. True or False: Jesus stopped a crowd from stoning a woman by writing on the ground.

9. True or False: Isaiah calls God a "God of justice."

10. True or False: Zacchaeus promised to repay those he cheated four times the amount.

Fill in the Blank:

11. Proverbs says, "Speak up for those who cannot _____ for themselves."

12. Jesus taught, "Blessed are the _____, for they will be shown mercy."

13. God told Israel, "Do not mistreat or oppress a _____, for you were _____ in Egypt."

14. The prophet Nathan confronted King _____ for his injustice toward Uriah.

15. Jesus quoted Hosea: "I desire mercy, not _____."

Who Said That?

16. "You intended to harm me, but God intended it for good."

   a) Joseph

   b) Moses

   c) Samuel

   d) Ezra

17. "Will not the Judge of all the earth do right?"

   a) Abraham

   b) Job

   c) David

   d) Habakkuk

Bible Book Breakdown:

18. The parable of the Good Samaritan appears in the Gospel of _____ (chapter 10).

19. Amos's justice-river quote is in Amos chapter _____.

Answers

Multiple Choice Missions

1. b) Amos

2. b) Good

3. b) Gleaning

4. b) Humbly

5. a) Abraham

True or False

6. True

7. False

8. True

9. True

10. True

Fill in the Blank

11. Speak

12. Merciful

13. foreigner/alien/stranger, foreigners/aliens/strangers

14. David

15. Sacrifice

Who Said That?

16. a) Joseph

17. a) Abraham

Bible Book Breakdown

18. Luke

19. 5

Part 8: Courage & Risk-Taking

Ever felt that knot in your stomach when you know you need to do something tough or step way out of your comfort zone? Many ordinary people in the Bible showed courage and took huge risks, not for fame, but for God.

Multiple Choice Missions:

1. Esther risked her life by approaching King _____ without being summoned.

    a) Nebuchadnezzar

    b) Ahasuerus/Xerxes

    c) Artaxerxes

    d) Darius

2. Which disciple leapt out of the boat to walk on water toward Jesus?

    a) Andrew

    b) Peter

    c) John

    d) Philip

3. Shadrach, Meshach, and Abednego stood up to worship a golden image under which king?

    a) Darius

    b) Belshazzar

    c) Nebuchadnezzar

    d) Cyrus

4. What young prophet confronted King David with a story about a stolen lamb?

    a) Gad

    b) Ahijah

    c) Nathan

    d) Samuel

5. Who hid the Israelite spies on Jericho's wall?

    a) Deborah

    b) Rahab

    c) Leah

    d) Miriam

True or False:

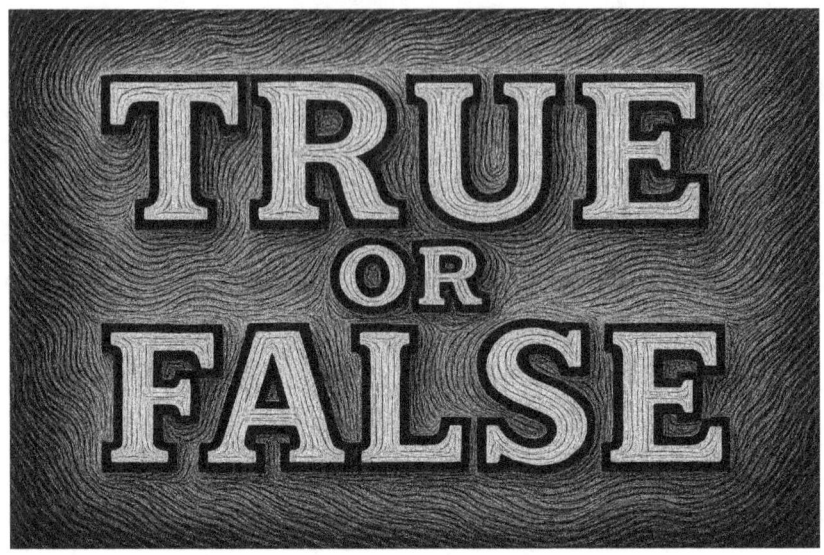

6. True or False: Jesus told Jairus, "Don't be afraid; just believe."

7. True or False: Gideon's first act of courage was destroying his father's Baal altar at night.

8. True or False: Stephen's bold sermon led directly to his immediate release.

9. True or False: Barnabas risked his reputation by introducing Saul/Paul to the Jerusalem church.

10. True or False: Moses first refused God's call because he feared public speaking.

Fill in the Blank:

11. The angel told Mary, "Do not be afraid, you have found _____ with God."

12. David told Goliath, "You come against me with sword and spear, but I come against you in the name of the _____ of Hosts."

13. After healing the lame man, Peter declared, "We must obey _____ rather than men."

14. Jonathan and his armor-bearer said, "Nothing can hinder the LORD from saving, whether by many or by _____."

15. Hebrews urges believers to "approach God's throne of grace with _____."

Who Said That?

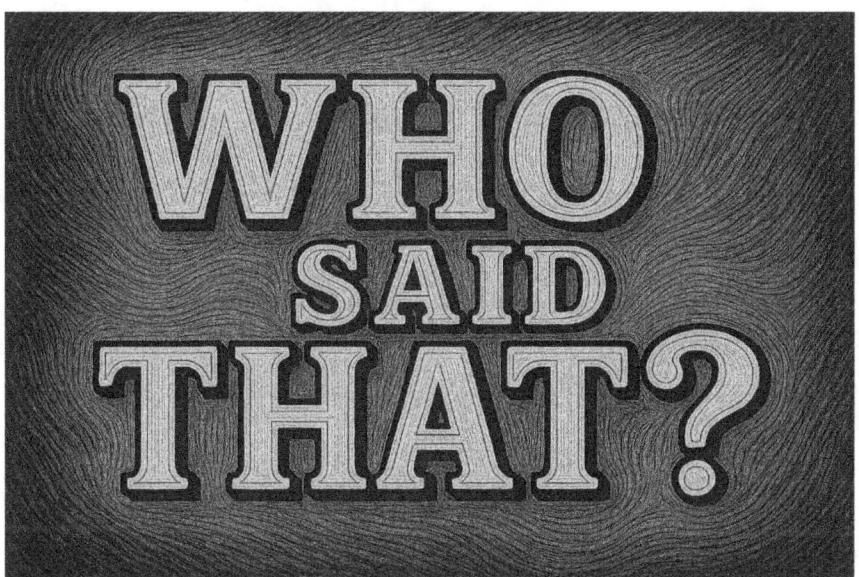

16. "Perhaps you have come to your royal position for such a time as this."

    a) Mordecai

    b) Haman

    c) Ezra

    d) Nehemiah

17. "Here am I. Send me!"

    a) Jeremiah

    b) Isaiah

    c) Ezekiel

    d) Elisha

Bible Book Breakdown:

18. Daniel's fiery-furnace story is in Daniel chapter _____.

19. Rahab's brave hiding mission shows up in the book of _____ (chapter 2).

Answers

Multiple Choice Missions

1. b) Ahasuerus/Xerxes

2. b) Peter

3. c) Nebuchadnezzar

4. c) Nathan

5. b) Rahab

True or False

6. True

7. True

8. False

9. True

10. True

Fill in the Blank

11. Favor

12. Lord

13. God

14. Few

15. confidence/boldness

Who Said That?

16. a) Mordecai

17. b) Isaiah

Bible Book Breakdown

18. 3

19. Joshua

Section 4 – Lightning Round (100 Rapid-Fire Questions)
(All multiple-choice; keep them quick!)

Have you been enjoying the quiz sections so far? Now, let's level up the challenge in the next couple of sections! Once you've written down your answers, you can scroll to the end of this book to get the answers.

1. The "abomination of desolation" phrase in Daniel 9 is quoted by Jesus in which chapter?

    a) Matthew 24

    b) Luke 21

    c) John 17

    d) Mark 11

2. Which Minor Prophet is almost identical in content to parts of Jeremiah?

    a) Nahum

    b) Obadiah

    c) Habakkuk

    d) Zephaniah

3. John's seven signs include turning water to wine and which final sign before the cross?

    a) Walking on water

    b) Raising Lazarus

    c) Feeding 5 000

    d) Healing blind man

4. Who served as governor of Judah during the rebuilding of the temple (Haggai 1)?

    a) Ezra

    b) Nehemiah

    c) Zerubbabel

    d) Sheshbazzar

5. Paul's "hymn of love" (agapē) appears in which chapter?

    a) Romans 8

    b) 1 Cor 13

    c) Eph 3

    d) Phil 2

6. Tribe that supplied Israel's line of priests?

    a) Judah

    b) Levi

    c) Benjamin

    d) Dan

7. Jesus healed ten lepers; how many returned to thank him?

    a) 1

    b) 3

    c) 5

    d) 10

8. King who found the Book of the Law during temple repairs?

    a) Hezekiah

    b) Josiah

    c) Jehoram

    d) Uzziah

9. Which letter mentions Melchizedek the most?

    a) Galatians

    b) Hebrews

    c) 1 Peter

    d) Colossians

10. What was the name of the city where disciples were first called "Christians"?

    a) Jerusalem

    b) Antioch

    c) Ephesus

    d) Corinth

11. Who was Israel's longest-reigning king?

    a) Manasseh

    b) David

    c) Hezekiah

    d) Zedekiah

12. Which gospel is shortest?

    a) Matthew

    b) Mark

    c) Luke

    d) John

13. What bird did Noah release second?

a) Dove

b) Raven

c) Sparrow

d) Eagle

14. Paul was shipwrecked on which island?

a) Crete

b) Malta

c) Cyprus

d) Patmos

15. How many chapters are in Psalms?

a) 100

b) 119

c) 150

d) 180

16. Who dreamed of a statue with four metals?

a) Daniel

b) Nebuchadnezzar

c) Joseph

d) Belshazzar

17. First miracle of Jesus?

a) Walking on water

b) Water to wine

c) Healing leper

d) Feeding 5 000

18. Book that ends "Grace be with all."

a) Revelation

b) Jude

c) Philemon

d) 3 John

19. Prophet who saw wheels within wheels?

    a) Isaiah

    b) Ezekiel

    c) Zechariah

    d) Malachi

20. How many spies did Moses send?

    a) 10

    b) 12

    c) 2

    d) 70

21. Jesus wept over which city?

    a) Bethany

    b) Jerusalem

    c) Capernaum

    d) Nazareth

22. Who was Moses' sister?

    a) Zipporah

    b) Miriam

    c) Hannah

    d) Deborah

23. The Beatitudes open which sermon?

    a) Mount

    b) Plain

    c) Temple

    d) Seaside

24. Oldest man in the Bible?

    a) Adam

    b) Seth

    c) Enoch

    d) Methuselah

25. Jacob's favorite son?

a) Reuben

b) Joseph

c) Benjamin

d) Judah

26. First Christian martyr?

a) James

b) Stephen

c) Peter

d) Paul

27. Plague #9 in Egypt?

a) Frogs

b) Locusts

c) Darkness

d) Hail

28. King with a writing on the wall?

a) Belshazzar

b) Darius

c) Xerxes

d) Ahab

29. Jesus' foster father's trade?

a) Fisherman

b) Carpenter

c) Farmer

d) Scribe

30. River Jordan parted for which prophet's cloak?

a) Samuel

b) Elisha

c) Jeremiah

d) Obadiah

31. Which judge of Israel was also a prophetess?

   a) Ruth

   b) Deborah

   c) Esther

   d) Jael

32. What was the name of the mountain where the Law was given to Moses?

   a) Mount Zion

   b) Mount Sinai

   c) Mount Carmel

   d) Mount of Olives

33. In the New Testament, who raised Tabitha (Dorcas) from the dead?

   a) Peter

   b) Paul

   c) John

   d) Luke

34. Which book of the Old Testament is a collection of love poems?

   a) Proverbs

   b) Ecclesiastes

   c) Song of Songs

   d) Lamentations

35. What was the name of the sorcerer who opposed Paul in Paphos?

   a) Simon Magus

   b) Bar-Jesus (Elymas)

   c) Apollos

   d) Barnabas

36. How many baskets of leftover food were collected after Jesus fed the 5,000?

   a) Seven

   b) Twelve

   c) Five

   d) Ten

37. Which Old Testament prophet is known for his visions of the end times, similar to Revelation?

    a) Amos

    b) Hosea

    c) Daniel

    d) Micah

38. What was the name of the garden where Jesus prayed before his crucifixion?

    a) Garden of Eden

    b) Garden of Gethsemane

    c) Mount of Olives

    d) Bethany

39. Who was the first Gentile convert recorded in the book of Acts?

    a) Lydia

    b) Cornelius

    c) Silas

    d) Timothy

40. Which book of the Old Testament expresses deep sorrow over the destruction of Jerusalem?

    a) Ezekiel

    b) Jeremiah

    c) Lamentations

    d) Habakkuk

41. What was the name of the angel who announced Jesus' birth to Mary?

    a) Michael

    b) Gabriel

    c) Raphael

    d) Uriel

42. Which of Paul's letters is addressed to the churches in Galatia?

    a) Philippians

    b) Ephesians

    c) Galatians

    d) Colossians

43. What was the occupation of Zacchaeus, whom Jesus called down from a tree?

    a) Fisherman

    b) Tax collector

    c) Carpenter

    d) Shepherd

44. Which Old Testament book contains the story of Shadrach, Meshach, and Abednego in the fiery furnace?

    a) Isaiah

    b) Jeremiah

    c) Daniel

    d) Ezekiel

45. What was the name of the first king of the divided kingdom of Israel (the northern kingdom)?

    a) Rehoboam

    b) Jeroboam

    c) Ahab

    d) Hoshea

46. Which book of the New Testament is a letter written by the brother of Jesus?

    a) 1 Peter

    b) 2 Peter

    c) James

    d) Jude

47. What was the name of the well where Jesus spoke to the Samaritan woman?

    a) Well of Abraham

    b) Jacob's Well

    c) Well of Isaac

    d) Well of Rebekah

48. Which Old Testament prophet used the analogy of a potter and clay to describe God's sovereignty?

   a) Isaiah

   b) Jeremiah

   c) Ezekiel

   d) Hosea

49. What was the name of the Roman centurion who declared, "Surely this man was the Son of God!"?

   a) Cornelius

   b) Longinus

   c) Julius

   d) Festus

50. Which book of the Old Testament is a collection of wisdom literature that questions the meaning of life?

   a) Proverbs

   b) Job

   c) Ecclesiastes

   d) Psalms

51. What was the name of Saul's general?

   a) Joab

   b) Abner

   c) Benaiah

   d) Adonijah

52. In what town did Jesus grow up?

   a) Bethlehem

   b) Nazareth

   c) Capernaum

   d) Jerusalem

53. Which of the following was NOT one of the gifts brought to the infant Jesus by the Magi?

   a) Gold

   b) Frankincense

   c) Myrrh

   d) Silver

54. What was the name of the short tax collector who climbed a sycamore-fig tree to see Jesus?

    a) Matthew

    b) Zacchaeus

    c) Levi

    d) Barnabas

55. Which Old Testament prophet was a shepherd and a fig-tree dresser?

    a) Amos

    b) Micah

    c) Hosea

    d) Joel

56. On what mountain did the transfiguration of Jesus occur?

    a) Mount Sinai

    b) Mount Hermon

    c) Mount Tabor

    d) Mount of Olives

57. Who was the Roman governor who presided over Paul's trial in Caesarea?

    a) Pontius Pilate

    b) Felix

    c) Festus

    d) Agrippa

58. What was the name of Abraham's nephew?

    a) Isaac

    b) Jacob

    c) Lot

    d) Ishmael

59. Which book of the Old Testament is a series of prophetic visions concerning the rebuilding of the temple and the coming Messiah?

    a) Haggai

    b) Zechariah

    c) Malachi

    d) Joel

60. What was the name of the pool in Jerusalem where Jesus healed a paralyzed man who had been lying there for 38 years?

    a) Pool of Siloam

    b) Pool of Bethesda

    c) Gihon Spring

    d) King's Pool

61. Who was the first wife of Jacob?

    a) Rachel

    b) Leah

    c) Bilhah

    d) Zilpah

62. Which of the following was NOT one of the signs given by Jesus in the Olivet Discourse concerning the end times?

    a) Wars and rumors of wars

    b) Famines and earthquakes

    c) A prolonged period of worldwide peace

    d) Persecution of believers

63. What was the name of the angel who appeared to Zechariah to announce the birth of John the Baptist?

    a) Michael

    b) Gabriel

    c) Raphael

    d) Uriel

64. Which book of the Old Testament contains the story of the writing on the wall during Belshazzar's feast?

    a) Ezekiel

    b) Daniel

    c) Isaiah

    d) Jeremiah

65. Who was the successor to the prophet Elijah?

    a) Elisha

    b) Micaiah

    c) Obadiah

    d) Habakkuk

66. What was the name of the town where Jesus performed his first miracle of turning water into wine?

    a) Bethany

    b) Cana

    c) Capernaum

    d) Nain

67. Which of Paul's letters was written to a church in a city famous for its temple dedicated to Artemis (Diana)?

    a) Philippians

    b) Colossians

    c) Ephesians

    d) 1 Thessalonians

68. What was the name of Isaac's wife?

    a) Sarah

    b) Rebekah

    c) Rachel

    d) Leah

69. Which of the following is NOT one of the major prophets in the Old Testament?

    a) Isaiah

    b) Jeremiah

    c) Ezekiel

    d) Amos

70. What was the name of the high priest who questioned Peter and John after the healing of the lame man at the temple gate?

    a) Annas

    b) Caiaphas

    c) Gamaliel

    d) Zadok

71. Who was the mother of Ishmael?

    a) Sarah

    b) Hagar

    c) Keturah

    d) Rebekah

72. Which of the following was NOT one of the temptations Jesus faced in the wilderness?

a) Turning stones into bread

b) Throwing himself down from the temple

c) Being offered all the kingdoms of the world

d) Being tempted to call down fire from heaven

73. What was the name of the Roman governor who interrogated Jesus before Pontius Pilate?

a) Herod Agrippa I

b) Herod Antipas

c) Felix

d) Festus

74. Which book of the Old Testament contains the story of Queen Vashti and Esther?

a) Ruth

b) Esther

c) Nehemiah

d) Ezra

75. Who was the disciple who replaced Judas Iscariot?

a) Barnabas

b) Silas

c) Matthias

d) Luke

76. What was the name of the town where Lazarus, Mary, and Martha lived?

a) Bethany

b) Capernaum

c) Jericho

d) Nain

77. Which of Paul's letters addresses issues of spiritual gifts and the resurrection?

    a) Philippians

    b) 2 Corinthians

    c) 1 Corinthians

    d) Ephesians

78. Who was the father of King David?

    a) Jesse

    b) Saul

    c) Jonathan

    d) Samuel

79. Which of the following is NOT one of the pastoral epistles?

    a) 1 Timothy

    b) 2 Timothy

    c) Titus

    d) Philemon

80. What was the name of the Sanhedrin member who provided his own tomb for Jesus' burial?

    a) Nicodemus

    b) Joseph of Arimathea

    c) Lazarus

    d) Zacchaeus

81. Who was the wife of Isaac?

    a) Sarah

    b) Rebekah

    c) Rachel

    d) Leah

82. Which of the following was NOT one of the miracles performed by Elisha?

    a) Raising a widow's son

    b) Healing Naaman's leprosy

    c) Turning water into wine

    d) Multiplying a widow's oil

83. What was the name of the proconsul of Cyprus who was converted after hearing Paul and Barnabas?

    a) Sergius Paulus

    b) Gallio

    c) Lysanias

    d) Erastus

84. Which book of the Old Testament contains the prophecies of Habakkuk?

    a) Amos

    b) Hosea

    c) Habakkuk

    d) Zephaniah

85. Who was the disciple who was a physician?

    a) Peter

    b) John

    c) Luke

    d) Matthew

86. What was the name of the town where Jesus raised a widow's son from the dead?

    a) Bethany

    b) Cana

    c) Capernaum

    d) Nain

87. Which of Paul's letters was written to a church in a city known for its philosophical schools?

    a) Philippians

    b) Colossians

    c) Thessalonica

    d) Corinth

88. Who was the father of John the Baptist?

    a) Zechariah

    b) Simeon

    c) Joseph

    d) Joachim

89. Which of the following is NOT one of the prison epistles?

a) Ephesians

b) Philippians

c) Colossians

d) 1 Thessalonians

90. What was the name of the high priest who questioned Jesus before the Sanhedrin along with Caiaphas?

a) Annas

b) Gamaliel

c) Zadok

d) Abiathar

91. Who was the mother of Jacob and Esau?

a) Sarah

b) Rebekah

c) Rachel

d) Leah

92. Which of the following was NOT one of the signs that occurred at Jesus' crucifixion?

a) Darkness over the land

b) An earthquake

c) The tearing of the temple curtain

d) A great storm at sea

93. What was the name of the governor who succeeded Felix in Judea and heard Paul's defense?

a) Pontius Pilate

b) Herod Agrippa II

c) Festus

d) Claudius Lysias

94. Which book of the Old Testament contains the prophecies of Haggai?

a) Zechariah

b) Malachi

c) Haggai

d) Obadiah

95. Who was the disciple who was a tax collector?

   a) Peter

   b) James

   c) Matthew

   d) John

96. What was the name of the town where the Apostle Paul was stoned and left for dead during his first missionary journey?

   a) Lystra

   b) Iconium

   c) Antioch of Pisidia

   d) Derbe

97. Which book of the Old Testament contains the prophecies of Malachi?

   a) Zechariah

   b) Haggai

   c) Malachi

   d) Joel

98. Who was the disciple who was known as "the one whom Jesus loved"?

   a) Peter

   b) James

   c) John

   d) Andrew

99. What was the name of the island to which the Apostle John was exiled when he wrote the book of Revelation?

   a) Malta

   b) Cyprus

   c) Patmos

   d) Crete

100. Which of the following Old Testament books is primarily a collection of wisdom sayings attributed to King Solomon?

   a) Ecclesiastes

   b) Job

   c) Proverbs

   d) Song of Songs

Answers

1. a) Matthew 24
2. b) Obadiah
3. b) Raising Lazarus
4. c) Zerubbabel
5. b) 1 Cor 13
6. b) Levi
7. a) 1
8. b) Josiah
9. b) Hebrews
10. b) Antioch
11. a) Manasseh
12. b) Mark
13. a) Dove
14. b) Malta
15. c) 150
16. b) Nebuchadnezzar
17. b) Water to wine
18. d) 3 John
19. b) Ezekiel
20. b) 12
21. b) Jerusalem
22. b) Miriam
23. a) Mount
24. d) Methuselah
25. b) Joseph
26. b) Stephen
27. c) Darkness
28. a) Belshazzar
29. b) Carpenter
30. b) Elisha
31. b) Deborah

52. b) Nazareth
53. d) Silver
54. b) Zacchaeus
55. a) Amos
56. c) Mount Tabor
57. b) Felix
58. c) Lot
59. b) Zechariah
60. b) Pool of Bethesda
61. b) Leah
62. c) A prolonged period of worldwide peace
63. b) Gabriel
64. b) Daniel
65. a) Elisha
66. b) Cana
67. c) Ephesians
68. b) Rebekah
69. d) Amos
70. a) Annas
71. b) Hagar
72. d) Being tempted to call down fire from heaven
73. b) Herod Antipas
74. b) Esther
75. c) Matthias
76. a) Bethany
77. c) 1 Corinthians
78. a) Jesse
79. d) Philemon
80. b) Joseph of Arimathea

32. b) Mount Sinai

33. a) Peter

34. c) Song of Songs

35. b) Bar-Jesus (Elymas)

36. b) Twelve

37. c) Daniel

38. b) Garden of Gethsemane

39. b) Cornelius

40. c) Lamentations

41. b) Gabriel

42. c) Galatians

43. b) Tax collector

44. c) Daniel

45. b) Jeroboam

46. c) James

47. b) Jacob's Well

48. b) Jeremiah

49. b) Longinus

50. c) Ecclesiastes

51. b) Abner

81. b) Rebekah

82. c) Turning water into wine

83. a) Sergius Paulus

84. c) Habakkuk

85. c) Luke

86. d) Nain

87. d) Corinth

88. a) Zechariah

89. d) 1 Thessalonians

90. a) Annas

91. b) Rebekah

92. d) A great storm at sea

93. c) Festus

94. c) Haggai

95. c) Matthew

96. a) Lystra

97. c) Malachi

98. c) John

99. c) Patmos

100. c) Proverbs

Section 5 – Ultimate Challenge

50 Fill in the Blank

1. "Man shall not live on _____ alone, but on every word that comes from the mouth of God."

2. After Elijah, _____ asked for a double portion of his spirit.

3. "Perfect love casts out _____."

4. The fruit of the Spirit listed in Galatians starts with "love, joy, _____."

5. Moses' face shone after he spoke with _____.

6. The shortest verse in English language Bibles: "Jesus _____."

7. The armor of God includes the breastplate of _____.

8. Revelation's final invitation says, "Let the one who is _____ come."

9. The Great Commission ends with "I am with you _____."

10. Rahab tied a _____ cord in her window.

11. "I have been crucified with Christ and I no longer live, but _____ lives in me."

12. Before becoming Paul, he was known by his Hebrew name, _____.

13. "For the wages of sin is _____ , but the gift of God is eternal life in Christ Jesus our Lord."

14. The Passover meal commemorates the Israelites' deliverance from slavery in _____.

15. The Old Testament prophet _____ had visions of a valley of dry bones.

16. "For where two or three gather in my name, there _____ I am with them."

17. The Apostle _____ wrote the book of Revelation while exiled on the island of Patmos.

18. The Old Testament book of _____ is a collection of wise sayings.

19. "Blessed are the _____ , for they will be comforted." (Matthew 5:4)

20. The city of _____ was destroyed by fire and brimstone because of its wickedness.

21. "The Lord is my shepherd; I shall not _____ ."

22. The Apostle _____ initially doubted Jesus' resurrection.

23. The Old Testament book of _____ tells the story of a man who lost everything but remained faithful to God.

24. "For all have sinned and fall short of the _____ of God."

25. The first miracle performed by the Apostle Peter after Pentecost was healing a lame man at the Beautiful Gate of the temple in _____.

26. "For God did not send his Son into the world to _____ the world, but to save the world through him."

27. The Old Testament prophet _____ challenged the prophets of Baal on Mount Carmel.

28. "_____ the Lord, all you nations; extol him, all you peoples." (Psalm 117:1)

29. The Apostle _____ wrote several letters, including those to the churches in Corinth.

30. The parable of the _____ and the tax collector highlights the importance of humility in prayer.

31. "The _____ of the Lord is the beginning of wisdom." (Psalm 111:10)

32. The Apostle _____ wrote the Gospel that emphasizes Jesus' divine nature.

33. The Old Testament book of _____ contains songs of worship and praise.

34. "For by grace you have been saved, through _____ —and this is not from yourselves, it is the gift of God."

35. The early Christian deacon _____ was stoned for his faith.

36. "I can do all things through _____ who strengthens me." (Philippians 4:13)

37. The Old Testament prophet _____ foretold the coming of a messenger who would prepare the way for the Lord.

38. "The steadfast love of the Lord never ceases; his _____ never come to an end." (Lamentations 3:22)

39. The Apostle _____ wrote letters that address issues of social justice and the rich and poor.

40. The parable of the _____ Seed illustrates the growth of the Kingdom of God.

41. "_____ to the Lord, for he is good; his love endures forever." (1 Chronicles 16:34)

42. The Apostle _____ was the brother of Jesus and wrote a letter emphasizing practical faith.

43. The Old Testament book of _____ tells the story of a prophet who was swallowed by a large fish.

44. "For where your _____ is, there your heart will be also." (Matthew 6:21)

45. The early Christian couple _____ and Priscilla were close associates of Paul.

46. "Be _____ in hope, patient in affliction, faithful in prayer." (Romans 12:12)

47. The Old Testament prophet _____ confronted King David about his sin with Bathsheba.

48. "The Lord bless you and _____ you; the Lord make his face shine on you and be gracious to you." (Numbers 6:24-25)

49. The Apostle _____ wrote letters that warn against false teachers and emphasize the importance of love.

50. The parable of the _____ Servant teaches about the importance of forgiveness.

Answers

1. "Man shall not live on **bread** alone, but on every word that comes from the mouth of God."

2. After Elijah, **Elisha** asked for a double portion of his spirit.

3. "Perfect love casts out **fear**."

4. The fruit of the Spirit listed in Galatians starts with "love, joy, **peace**."

5. Moses' face shone after he spoke with **God**.

6. The shortest verse in English Bibles: "Jesus **wept**."

7. The armor of God includes the breastplate of **righteousness**.

8. Revelation's final invitation says, "Let the one who is **thirsty** come."

9. The Great Commission ends with "I am with you **always**."

10. Rahab tied a **scarlet** cord in her window.

11. "I have been crucified with Christ and I no longer live, but **Christ** lives in me."

12. Before becoming Paul, he was known by his Hebrew name, **Saul**.

13. "For the wages of sin is **death**, but the gift of God is eternal life in Christ Jesus our Lord."

14. The Passover meal commemorates the Israelites' deliverance from slavery in **Egypt**.

15. The Old Testament prophet **Ezekiel** had visions of a valley of dry bones.

16. "For where two or three gather in my name, there **I** am with them."

17. The Apostle **John** wrote the book of Revelation while exiled on the island of Patmos.

18. The Old Testament book of **Proverbs** is a collection of wise sayings.

19. "Blessed are the **meek**, for they will be comforted." (Matthew 5:4)

20. The city of **Sodom** was destroyed by fire and brimstone because of its wickedness.

21. "The Lord is my shepherd; I shall not **want**."

22. The Apostle **Thomas** initially doubted Jesus' resurrection.

23. The Old Testament book of **Job** tells the story of a man who lost everything but remained faithful to God.

24. "For all have sinned and fall short of the **glory** of God."

25. The first miracle performed by the Apostle Peter after Pentecost was healing a lame man at the Beautiful Gate of the temple in **Jerusalem**.

26. "For God did not send his Son into the world to **condemn** the world, but to save the world through him."

27. The Old Testament prophet **Elijah** challenged the prophets of Baal on Mount Carmel.

28. "**Praise** the Lord, all you nations; extol him, all you peoples." (Psalm 117:1)

29. The Apostle **Paul** wrote several letters, including those to the churches in Corinth.

30. The parable of the **Pharisee** and the tax collector highlights the importance of humility in prayer.

31. "The **fear** of the Lord is the beginning of wisdom." (Psalm 111:10)

32. The Apostle **John** wrote the Gospel that emphasizes Jesus' divine nature.

33. The Old Testament book of **Psalms** contains songs of worship and praise.

34. "For by grace you have been saved, through **faith**—and this is not from yourselves, it is the gift of God."

35. The early Christian deacon **Stephen** was stoned for his faith.

36. "I can do all things through **Christ** who strengthens me." (Philippians 4:13)

37. The Old Testament prophet **Malachi** foretold the coming of a messenger who would prepare the way for the Lord.

38. "The steadfast love of the Lord never ceases; his **mercies** never come to an end." (Lamentations 3:22)

39. The Apostle **James** wrote letters that address issues of social justice and the rich and poor.

40. The parable of the **mustard** Seed illustrates the growth of the Kingdom of God.

41. "**Give thanks** to the Lord, for he is good; his love endures forever." (1 Chronicles 16:34)

42. The Apostle **James** was the brother of Jesus and wrote a letter emphasizing practical faith.

43. The Old Testament book of **Jonah** tells the story of a prophet who was swallowed by a large fish.

44. "For where your **treasure** is, there your heart will be also." (Matthew 6:21)

45. The early Christian couple **Aquila** and Priscilla were close associates of Paul.

46. "Be **joyful** in hope, patient in affliction, faithful in prayer." (Romans 12:12)

47. The Old Testament prophet **Nathan** confronted King David about his sin with Bathsheba.

48. "The Lord bless you and **keep** you; the Lord make his face shine on you and be gracious to you." (Numbers 6:24-25)

49. The Apostle **John** wrote letters that warn against false teachers and emphasize the importance of love.

50. The parable of the **Unforgiving** Servant teaches about the importance of forgiveness.

Who Said That?

1. "My God, my God, why have you forsaken me?"

2. "Can these dry bones live?"

3. "We must obey God rather than human beings!"

4. "I am the way and the truth and the life. No one comes to the Father except through me."

5. "The spirit of the Lord is on me, because he has anointed me to proclaim good news to the poor."

6. "Where you go I will go, and where you stay I will stay. Your people will be my people and your God my God."

7. "Look, the Lamb of God, who takes away the sin of the world!"

8. "Silver or gold I do not have, but what I do have I give you. In the name of Jesus Christ of Nazareth, walk."

9. "Do not be afraid; keep on speaking, do not be silent."

10. "How long will you waver between two opinions? If the Lord is God, follow him; but if Baal is God, follow him."

11. "Unless I see the nail marks in his hands and put my finger where the nails were, and put my hand into his side, I will not believe."

12. "You are the Christ, the Son of the living God."

13. "I am not ashamed of the gospel, because it is the power of God that brings salvation to everyone who believes."

14. "Woe to me if I do not preach the gospel!"

15. "Our hearts are restless until they rest in you." (Attributed to Augustine, reflecting biblical themes)

16. "The kingdom of God is not a matter of eating and drinking, but of righteousness, peace and joy in the Holy Spirit."

17. "I have fought the good fight, I have finished the race, I have kept the faith."

18. "For everything there is a season, and a time for every matter under heaven."

19. "I know that my redeemer lives, and that in the end he will stand upon the earth."

20. "As for me and my household, we will serve the Lord."

21. "The Lord is my strength and my shield; in him my heart trusts, and I am helped; my heart exults, and with my song I give thanks to him."

Answers

1. "My God, my God, why have you forsaken me?" - **Jesus**

2. "Can these dry bones live?" - **Ezekiel**

3. "We must obey God rather than human beings!" - **Peter and the other apostles**

4. "I am the way and the truth and the life. No one comes to the Father except through me." - **Jesus**

5. "The Spirit of the Lord is on me, because he has anointed me to proclaim good news to the poor." - **Jesus**

6. "Where you go I will go, and where you stay I will stay. Your people will be my people and your God my God." - **Ruth**

7. "Look, the Lamb of God, who takes away the sin of the world!" - **John the Baptist**

8. "Silver or gold I do not have, but what I do have I give you. In the name of Jesus Christ of Nazareth, walk." - **Peter**

9. "Do not be afraid; keep on speaking, do not be silent." - **The Lord to Paul**

10. "How long will you waver between two opinions? If the Lord is God, follow him; but if Baal is God, follow him." - **Elijah**

11. "Unless I see the nail marks in his hands and put my finger where the nails were, and put my hand into his side, I will not believe." - **Thomas**

12. "You are the Christ, the Son of the living God." - **Peter**

13. "I am not ashamed of the gospel, because it is the power of God that brings salvation to everyone who believes." - **Paul**

14. "Woe to me if I do not preach the gospel!" - **Paul**

15. "Our hearts are restless until they rest in you." (Attributed to Augustine, reflecting biblical themes) - **Augustine**

16. "The kingdom of God is not a matter of eating and drinking, but of righteousness, peace and joy in the Holy Spirit." - **Paul**

17. "I have fought the good fight, I have finished the race, I have kept the faith." - **Paul**

18. "For everything there is a season, and a time for every matter under heaven." - **Solomon (Ecclesiastes)**

19. "I know that my redeemer lives, and that in the end he will stand upon the earth." - **Job**

20. "As for me and my household, we will serve the Lord." - **Joshua**

21. "The Lord is my strength and my shield; in him my heart trusts, and I am helped; my heart exults, and with my song I give thanks to him." - **David**

Extra Round: Women of the Word (50 Questions)

Part 1: Old Testament (20 Questions)

1. Who was the first woman mentioned by name in the Bible?

   a) Eve

   b) Sarah

   c) Rebekah

   d) Hagar

2. Which woman was known for her beauty and became the queen of Persia?

   a) Ruth

   b) Esther

   c) Deborah

   d) Rahab

3. Who was the mother of Samuel and prayed fervently for a child?

   a) Hannah

   b) Rachel

   c) Leah

   d) Rebekah

4. Which woman showed great loyalty to her mother-in-law Naomi?

   a) Orpah

   b) Ruth

   c) Michal

   d) Abigail

5. Who was the famous prophetess and judge?

   a) Miriam

   b) Deborah

   c) Huldah

   d) Noadiah

6. Which woman helped to save spies and her family during the fall of Jericho?

   a) Rahab

   b) Jael

   c) Delilah

   d) Rizpah

7. Who was the wife of Abraham?

   a) Hagar

   b) Keturah

   c) Sarah

   d) Milcah

8. Which woman was known for her wisdom and advised King David?

   a) Bathsheba

   b) Tamar

   c) Abigail

   d) Jezebel

9. Who was the sister of Moses and Aaron?

   a) Zipporah

   b) Elisheba

   c) Miriam

   d) Puah

10. Which woman was tricked into marrying Jacob?

    a) Rachel

    b) Leah

    c) Bilhah

    d) Zilpah

11. What was the name of Samson's mother?

    a) Zillah

    b) Manoah's wife (unnamed)

    c) Naamah

    d) Abital

12. Which woman was the wife of Isaac?

    a) Rachel

    b) Leah

    c) Rebekah

    d) Bilhah

13. Which woman was the mother of Joeph and Benjamin?

    a) Bilhah

    b) Zilpah

    c) Leah

    d) Rachel

14. Who was the only daughter of Jacob mentioned by name?

    a) Dinah

    b) Serah

    c) Asenath

    d) Jochebed

15. Which woman was the mother of Moses?

    a) Jochebed

    b) Shiprah

    c) Puah

    d) Elisheba

16. Which woman was the wife of King Ahab and known for her wickedness?

   a) Jezebel

   b) Athaliah

   c) Gomer

   d) Maacah

17. Which woman was the wife of Hosea?

   a) Gomer

   b) Rizpah

   c) Noadiah

   d) Anath

18. Which woman was known for cutting off Sisera's head with a tent peg?

   a) Deborah

   b) Jael

   c) Barak's wife (unnamed)

   d) Abishag

19. Which woman was the mother of King Solomon?

   a) Michal

   b) Bathsheba

   c) Haggith

   d) Abishag

20. Which woman was the daughter of Jephthah who mourned her virginity?

   a) Jephthah's daughter (unnamed)

   b) Iscah

   c) Milcah

   d) Maacah

Answers

1. a) Eve
2. b) Esther
3. a) Hannah
4. b) Ruth
5. b) Deborah
6. a) Rahab
7. c) Sarah
8. c) Abigail
9. c) Miriam
10. b) Leah
11. b) Manoah's wife (unnamed)
12. c) Rebekah
13. d) Rachel
14. a) Dinah
15. a) Jochebed
16. a) Jezebel
17. a) Gomer
18. b) Jael
19. b) Bathsheba
20. a) Jephthah's daughter (unnamed)

Part 2: New Testament (20 Questions)

21. Who was the mother of Jesus?

    a) Elizabeth

    b) Mary

    c) Salome

    d) Susanna

22. Which woman was the first to see Jesus after his resurrection?

    a) Mary Magdalene

    b) Mary, the mother of James

    c) Joanna

    d) Salome

23. Who was the sister of Martha and Lazarus?

    a) Mary

    b) Martha

    c) Salome

    d) Susanna

24. Which woman was known for her hospitality to Jesus?

    a) Mary Magdalene

    b) Mary, the mother of James

    c) Martha

    d) Joanna

25. Who was the mother of John the Baptist?

    a) Mary

    b) Elizabeth

    c) Anna

    d) Salome

26. Which woman was a prophetess who recognized Jesus as the Messiah in the temple?

    a) Mary

    b) Elizabeth

    c) Anna

    d) Priscilla

27. Which woman was a prominent leader in the early church and a tentmaker?

    a) Lydia

    b) Phoebe

    c) Junia

    d) Priscilla

28. Which woman was known for her generosity and hospitality in Philippi?

    a) Lydia

    b) Phoebe

    c) Junia

    d) Chloe

29. Which woman was commended by Paul as a deaconess or servant of the church?

    a) Lydia

    b) Phoebe

    c) Junia

    d) Tryphena

30. Which woman is mentioned in Romans 16 as being outstanding among the apostles?

    a) Lydia

    b) Phoebe

    c) Junia

    d) Persis

31. Who was the wife of Herod Antipas, who demanded the head of John the Baptist?

    a) Joanna

    b) Susanna

    c) Salome

    d) Herodias

32. Who was the daughter of Herodias, who danced for Herod and requested John the Baptist's head?

   a) Salome

   b) Drusilla

   c) Bernice

   d) Lydia

33. Which woman was healed by Jesus after suffering from bleeding for twelve years?

   a) Mary Magdalene

   b) Mary, the mother of James

   c) The woman with the issue of blood (unnamed)

   d) Susanna

34. Who was the wife of Zechariah and mother of John the Baptist?

   a) Mary

   b) Elizabeth

   c) Anna

   d) Salome

35. Which woman was a follower of Jesus and provided for his ministry out of her means?

   a) Mary Magdalene

   b) Joanna

   c) Susanna

   d) Mary, the mother of James

36. Which woman was the wife of Aquila and a fellow tentmaker with Paul?

   a) Phoebe

   b) Priscilla

   c) Junia

   d) Tryphena

37. Which woman is mentioned in Romans 16 as a beloved Christian worker?

　　a) Persis

　　b) Julia

　　c) Nereus' sister (unnamed)

　　d) Rufus' mother (unnamed)

38. Which woman is mentioned in Romans 16 as a chosen lady?

　　a) Elect lady (unnamed)

　　b) Tryphaena

　　c) Tryphosa

　　d) Julia

39. Which two women are mentioned in Romans 16 as workers in the Lord?

　　a) Mary and Persis

　　b) Tryphaena and Tryphosa

　　c) Julia and Nereus' sister

　　d) Rufus' mother and his sister

40. Which woman is mentioned in Romans 16 as the mother of Rufus and someone who was also a mother to Paul?

　　a) Julia

　　b) Tryphaena

　　c) Rufus' mother (unnamed)

　　d) Persis

Answers

21. b) Mary

22. a) Mary Magdalene

23. a) Mary

24. c) Martha

25. b) Elizabeth

26. c) Anna

27. d) Priscilla

28. a) Lydia

29. b) Phoebe

30. c) Junia

31. d) Herodias

32. a) Salome

33. c) The woman with the issue of blood (unnamed)

34. b) Elizabeth

35. b) Joanna

36. b) Priscilla

37. a) Persis

38. a) Elect lady (unnamed)

39. b) Tryphaena and Tryphosa

40. c) Rufus' mother (unnamed)

Part 3: Who Said That? (5 Questions)

41. "Where you go I will go, and where you stay I will stay. Your people will be my people and your God my God."

    a) Sarah

    b) Ruth

    c) Esther

    d) Hannah

42. "My soul glorifies the Lord and my spirit rejoices in God my Savior."

    a) Elizabeth

    b) Mary

    c) Anna

    d) Priscilla

43. "Do whatever he tells you."

    a) Mary (mother of Jesus)

    b) Martha

    c) Mary Magdalene

    d) Salome

44. "If I perish, I perish."

    a) Ruth

    b) Rahab

    c) Esther

    d) Jael

45. "For this child I prayed; and the Lord hath given me my petition which I asked of him"

    a) Sarah

    b) Rebekah

    c) Rachel

    d) Hannah

Answers

41. b) Ruth
42. b) Mary
43. a) Mary (mother of Jesus)
44. c) Esther
45. d) Hannah

Part 4: Fill in the Blank (5 Questions)

46. "Charm is deceptive, and beauty is fleeting; but a woman who fears the LORD is to be _____." (Proverbs 31:30, NKJV)

47. "Then God said, 'It is not good that the _____ should be alone; I will make him a helper comparable to him.' (Genesis 2:18, NKJV)

48. "And without faith it is impossible to please him, for whoever would draw near to God must believe that he exists and that he _____ those who seek him." (Hebrews 11:6, NKJV)

49. "But the fruit of the Spirit is love, joy, peace, forbearance, kindness, goodness, faithfulness, gentleness, _____." (Galatians 5:22-23, NIV)

50. "There is neither Jew nor Gentile, neither slave nor free, nor is there male and _____, for you are all one in Christ Jesus." (Galatians 3:28, NIV)

Answers

46. praised
47. man
48. rewards
49. self-control
50. woman

SCORE CARD

NAME	SECTION	SCORE

Check out another book in the series

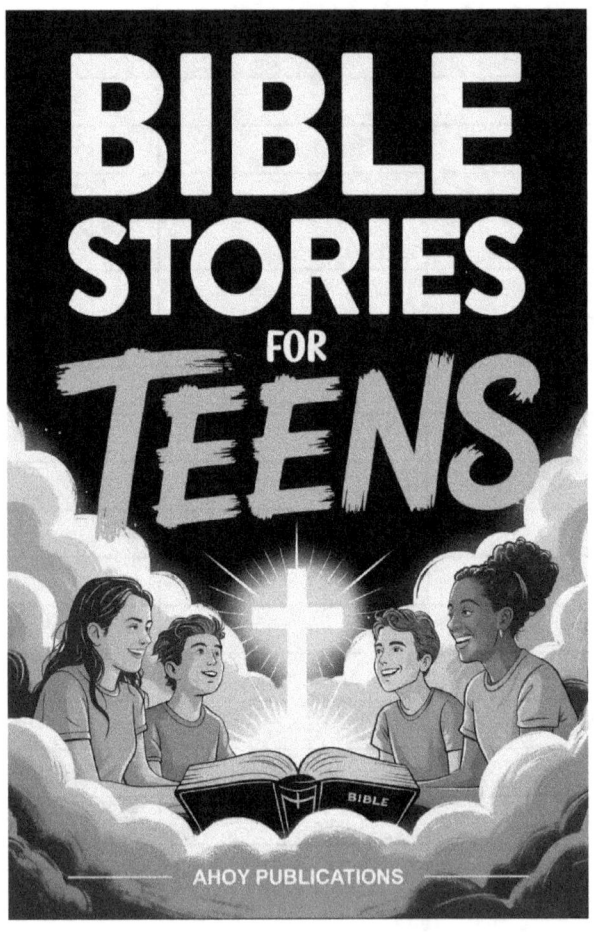

Welcome Aboard, Check Out This Limited-Time Free Bonus!

Ahoy, reader! Welcome to the Ahoy Publications family, and thanks for snagging a copy of this book! Since you've chosen to join us on this journey, we'd like to offer you something special.

Check out the link below for a FREE e-book filled with delightful facts about American History.

But that's not all - you'll also have access to our exclusive email list with even more free e-books and insider knowledge. Well, what are ye waiting for? Click the link below to join and set sail toward exciting adventures in American History.

Access your bonus here

https://ahoypublications.com/

Or, Scan the QR code!

www.ingramcontent.com/pod-product-compliance
Lightning Source LLC
Chambersburg PA
CBHW061801120626
46550CB00005B/2091